Lucky for Some
by John Dole

SERVING THEATRE

SINCE 1830

WWW.SAMUELFRENCH.CO.UK
WWW.SAMUELFRENCH.COM

FOR AMATEUR PRODUCTION ENQUIRIES

UNITED KINGDOM AND WORLD EXCLUDING NORTH AMERICA

plays@SamuelFrench-London.co.uk

020 7255 4302/01

Each title is subject to availability from Samuel French, depending upon country of performance.

CHARACTERS

MRS. CURTAIN

HORACE SPROGGS

MARY CLIFFORD

CHRISTOPHER CLIFFORD

MRS. LOTT

TOM LOTT

BUBBLES LAVERNE

ERNIE HIGGINS

MISS BOUNCE

SCENE:	A holiday camp chalet.*
TIME:	The present.
ACT ONE	A late evening in summer
ACT TWO	Very early the next morning
ACT THREE	Late the same day

* ANY RESEMBLANCE TO ANY ACTUAL HOLIDAY CAMP, LIVELY OR DEADLY, IS PURELY COINCIDENTAL.

Printed in Great Britain by offset lithography by
Billing & Sons Limited, Guildford and London

237 49507 4   PR. 4692

To Patricia

LUCKY FOR SOME

ACT ONE

A late evening in summer. The sun has set but there is enough light lingering in the sky outside, supplemented by a near-by lamp-post, to show us the interior of a rather barren room. There are three doors. The main one U.R. leads directly out into the open air; a second D.L. has the letters "N.C.O." painted in white on three little blocks; and a third and smaller door D.R. leads into a large cupboard. A window U.L., with modernistic curtains, looks out onto the side of what appears to be a barrack hut. The window is open. Immediately below the window stands a large double bed covered with a bright puce bedspread. U.R. in the corner is an old round stove with a pipe leading up through the roof. On either side of the bed a small commode-like bedside cupboard. Between the right-hand one and the door an uncomfort-able wooden chair. C.L. another chair to match and C.R. a decrepit armchair. Against the R. wall a folding screen about five feet high. Hanging on the hook R. of the main door a large football rattle over a notice which reads "Fire - Emergency Only".

The general decor is not inspiring. The walls up to eye level are painted green but above that appear to be bare boards. Some attempt has been made to cheer the place up with a couple of pictures but the choice is peculiar. One picture R.C. seems to have been borrowed from an old railway carriage and is probably a view of Bude on a foggy day in 1900. The other L.C. is a replica of Kitchener's famous 'The Army Needs You' recruiting poster.

On the wall above the main door is a Tannoy loud-speaker.

The overall first impression is of a barrack hut with trimmings.

Possibly a WRAC hut. And yet those curtains at the window and the bedspread surely can't be standard issue.

> When the Curtain rises the hut is empty but there are barrack square noises from outside; marching feet and an occasional high-pitched bark which could very well be the Company Sergeant Major in good voice.

> Suddenly the door U.R. bursts open and MRS. CURTAIN appears. She is a lady of indeterminate years. As common as couch-grass and just about as tenacious. She is wearing a pinafore and slippers and her hair is done up in a scarf which fails to conceal a lovely head of curlers. She carries a large handbell. The whole ensemble is set off by a large red sash emblazoned with the words 'Camp Hostess'.

> She flicks on the light switch by the door and a solitary bulb blinks to life in the middle of the hut under cover of a small dirty white shade. She takes up an aggressive position, rings the hand-bell violently and shouts at the top of a very loud and raucous voice - -

MRS. C.   Eyes down! Number one! Top of the shop! We've just begun!

> (She rings her bell again and goes out, closing the door behind her. As the echoes die away a grey-haired, stooped figure is seen crossing outside the window apparently bowed down by some very heavy weight. This is HORACE SPROGGS. He kicks open the door, puts down one of the suitcases he is carrying and peers short-sightedly at the Number "13" on the door. This is painted in large white figures on a piece of wood which hangs from a screw in the outside of the door. He gives a satisfied grunt, picks up the case and staggers stiffly and painfully into the room, and D.R. where he apparently gets stuck, blinking occasionally like a large, rather scruffy owl. He is wearing striped trousers and a tail-coat but the effect is badly undermined by the large woolly muffler wound round his neck and the commissionaire's cap with the words 'Sandpiper Camp' round the ribbon. Hanging on a string round his neck is a whistle. Voices are heard outside.)

MARY   (off)   I think he went this way.

CHRIS   (off)   He can't have got far. He was nearly out of gas.

(MARY appears outside the window.)

MARY   (looking back)   It's your fault if we've lost him.
You shouldn't have stopped at that ice-cream stall.

(CHRISTOPHER joins her outside the window.)

CHRIS   How was I to know he'd go galloping on? Anyway I
only stopped to ask the girl if she had an ice Tutti
Frutti.

MARY   I don't wonder she slapped your face.   (She peers
in through the window and spots HORACE.)   Here
he is, in here. Come on.   (She enters and moves
L.C. inspecting the premises with a jaundiced eye.
She is young, vivacious and pretty. Reasonably
well dressed but unsophisticated and not altogether
sure of herself. This shows from time to time in
her usually unjustified suspicions of CHRISTOPHER,
whose activities are more extraordinary than extra-
marital. She carries a smart handbag and is wearing a summery dress.

Outside there is a good deal of banging about and
CHRISTOPHER squeezes through the door backwards.
He is carrying a variety of sports gear - golf-clubs
in a bag, two tennis racquets, a fishing rod, a
haversack and a car blanket. He wears a broad-
brimmed sombrero well down over his ears, sun-
glasses, a striped blazer and flabby white shorts
which come down well below the knee. He is not a
romantic sight.

Having negotiated the doorway he stands breathing
heavily to recuperate.)

MARY   (indicating the room generally)   Is this it?

CHRIS   (peering round) I hope so. I'm about all in.

MARY   (walking round)   It didn't look like this in the
brochure.

CHRIS   They use a telephoto lens. It's a bit dark, isn't it?

MARY   (going to him)   You're wearing your blinkers.
(She removes his sun-glasses and puts them into
his breast pocket.)

CHRIS   Eh? Oh thanks.   (He blinks in the sudden light.)
I thought we were in for a storm.   (He sees
HORACE who is standing motionless D.R.)   I

didn't know we were sharing with anyone.

MARY   Don't be silly, darling. He's the porter.

CHRIS   (moving closer to inspect HORACE)   So that's why
              he's got a whistle. Can he talk?

              (HORACE goes into a sudden paroxysm of subterran-
              ean coughing, puts down the cases and blows his
              whistle which makes CHRISTOPHER jump. He picks
              up the cases again and speaks in a very hoarse voice
              looking straight ahead without the least trace of
              expression.)

HORACE   Welcome to the Sandpiper 'Oliday Camp.

MARY   How nice.

HORACE   (taking no notice)   They calls it that because it's
              a bit rough on the surface. I'm 'Orace.

CHRIS   (trying to fish in his pocket)   Yes, you are a bit.
              Try one of these cough-drops. They're very good –

HORACE   'Orace Sproggs. I'm standing in for the regular
              porter. 'E's down with food poisoning.

MARY   That sounds promising. It's pretty dismal here, isn't
              it?

HORACE   Yus, but it's very 'ealthy.   (He coughs again chest-
              ily.)   Air like wine.

              (CHRISTOPHER dumps his kit in a heap on the floor
              D.R. except for his bag of golf-clubs which he props
              in the armchair.)

CHRIS   Yes, I know, and sea like beer – brown and bitter.
              You'd better let me have those before you do your-
              self a mischief.   (He takes the two cases from
              HORACE's nerveless hands and tosses them lightly
              onto the bed.)

MARY   Are you sure this is the right place? It's so bare.

              (HORACE hobbles across to her taking a scruffy
              piece of paper out of his pocket.)

HORACE   Yus. Number Fourteen. That's what it says on yer
              chitty. Row Haitch Number Fourteen, see?   (He
              thrusts his paper under her nose.)

CHRIS   (going to the door)   Hey. Wait a minute. This is
              Number Thirteen. You've got it wrong.   (He points

to the number on the door.)

HORACE   No it ain't. It's Fourteen.

CHRIS   But it says Firteen – er – Thirteen on the door.

HORACE   I know. I know. Think I can't read? We 'ave to
         keep changing the number-boards round 'cause people
         are superstishus.

MARY   Then how do you know which hut is which? They all
         look alike to me.

HORACE   They ain't 'uts – they're shallys.   ·

MARY   All right, then – chalets. But I still don't see how
         you know which is which if the numbers get changed.

HORACE   'Cause Fourteen's Puce.

         (CHRISTOPHER and MARY look round at the green
         paint.)

CHRIS   Puce?

HORACE   (pointing)   The bedspread. It's puce, see?
         Firteen's yeller.

CHRIS   Oh!   (To MARY)   Firteen's yeller.

         (HORACE takes two lapel badges from his pocket and
         gives them to CHRISTOPHER.)

         What are these? Sleeping pills?

HORACE   Them's yer blood-chits. Don't ferget to wear 'em or
         you might lose yer whereabouts and get slung out on
         yer ear.   (He hobbles D.L.)

CHRIS   I read about a man once who wandered into a harem and
         lost his whereabouts.   (He pretends to read his
         badge.)   Mine says 'Kiss me Quick'.   (He nuzzles
         the back of MARY's neck.)

MARY   Don't play the fool.

         (CHRISTOPHER pins the badges onto his hat so that
         they look like eyes. He lays it on the armchair.
         HORACE meanwhile has opened the door D.L. and
         jerks his head towards the dark interior.)

HORACE   Wash-'ouse.

MARY   I beg your pardon?

HORACE   Wash-'ouse. Hablutions. Privileged you are. They
         'aven't all got running water laid on.

CHRIS   It must be the tidal suite.

         (MARY goes off D.L. switching on the light inside.
         HORACE sidles up to CHRISTOPHER.)

HORACE   'Ere! You ain't just got married, 'ave yer?

CHRIS   Good lord no. We're pros. Been married a year.

HORACE   That's all right then. I didn't think you 'ad that
         gooey look. We 'ave a 'ell of a time with them newly-
         weds. They gets in the way when we comes to make
         the beds.

CHRIS   Nuisance.

HORACE   And they won't join in the fun and games neither. I
         dunno why they bother to come away on 'oliday. Just
         sit around mooning.

         (MARY appears unexpectedly at the window.)

CHRIS   I expect that's why they call them honeymooners.
         (To MARY)   We didn't do that did we, darling –
         Hey! How did you get out there? Down the plug?

HORACE   There's a back way out through the wash-'ouse.

CHRIS   That'll be fun for visitors when we're having a quick
         tub.   (He peers into the bathroom and shuts the
         door.)

MARY   (pointing)   Why has it got those letters on the door?

HORACE   Ah! That's a relict, that is. This used to be an old
         Army camp, you see, until we took it over and rele-
         gated it.

CHRIS   Is that what happened to it?

HORACE   Yus. You know. We gave it a face lift. That's when
         we put in the barth. We left the old sign up as a
         warning.

MARY   A warning?

HORACE   (hobbling D.R.)   Yus. The lock's busted.

CHRIS   I still don't quite see what –

HORACE   (to MARY)   'E's a bit dim, isn't 'e? N.C.O. –
         No Clothes On. See?   (He raps on the door D.R.)
         And this 'ere was where they kept their rifles and

ammunition.

CHRIS   A sort of arsenal.

HORACE   Sort of.

MARY   (entering U.R.)   I hope they haven't left any relics in there.

HORACE   Naow! Bare as a baby's bottom. You can use it to 'ang yer clothes up.

CHRIS   And what about meals?

HORACE   Oh no. There ain't room to eat in there. Not unless you stick to celery. (He goes into a fit of subterranean laughter.)

CHRIS   I meant when do we eat?

HORACE   You'll 'ear all about that on the wireless. Stick to celery! He! he! (He goes into another paroxysm.)

CHRIS   Wireless?

HORACE   (pointing to Tannoy)   On the speaker.

CHRIS   Oh, I see. A sort of noshing forecast.

HORACE   That's right. And don't be late arriving at the dining 'all or somebody'll pinch yer butter. Yer irons are in the cupboard. (He points to the small cupboard L. of the bed and hobbles to the door U.R.)

MARY   Oh, we shan't need an iron. Everything's nylon.

HORACE   (shaking his head)   I dunno. They don't teach them nothing nowadays. Irons. You know – (And he makes eating motions.)   Oh yes, and that there's the stove but you can't use it before November.

MARY   Charming!

HORACE   (opening the door U.R.)   Well, it makes a nice ventilator. Oh, I nearly forgot. (He reaches out and brings in a red bucket of water apparently marked SAND.)   Just in case you're wondering. This 'ere's for fires.

CHRIS   Good lord. We shan't need a fire. It's summer.

HORACE   It ain't to put 'em in. It's to put 'em out. We're very 'ot on fires in this place.

MARY   You would be.

CHRIS   (looking in the pail)   It's full of water.

HORACE	What did you expect - tomato juice?
CHRIS	Well, seeing as it's marked 'SAND' I'd have expected sand.

(HORACE turns the bucket round - on the back is 'PIPER'.)

Sorry!

HORACE   We 'ave a fire drill every now and again. Keeps us lively.   (He gives CHRISTOPHER a hard look and returns the bucket outside the door.)

MARY   I wonder you don't issue us all with life-jackets. Then we could all have life-boat drill as well.

HORACE   (back in the room)   We never thought of that. I'll put your suggestion before the Entertainments Committee.

MARY   Talking of Entertainments, what are we supposed to do for amusement? I mean when we've finished playing firemen.

HORACE   You 'ollers for me.

CHRIS   And I suppose you come racing along at breakneck speed and tell us a funny story.

HORACE   That's right. You've 'eard of them Redcoats they 'ave at Billy Butlins - well, I'm a Blackcoat.
(He chants in a miserable voice.)
The Blackcoats are 'ere to see you get
An 'oliday as you won't ferget.
Whether you come from near or far -

CHRIS   We'll finish you off with a ra! ra! ra!
Don't call us. We'll call you.

HORACE   Won't do no good calling me tonight 'cause I'm off duty.   (He starts to leave.)

CHRIS   But what shall I do with all this gear?   (He points at the heap on the floor.)

HORACE   (indicating the door D.R.)   Stick it in the arsenal. (He goes out.)

(CHRISTOPHER takes a golf-club out of the bag and a ball from his blazer pocket. He tees up facing towards the audience.)

CHRIS   (cheerily)   Well, here we are. Beside the jolly old sea. Hot and cold running sand in every sock.

(MARY is examining the pictures critically.)

MARY   Honestly, Christopher, I don't know how you could.

CHRIS   How I could what? Like sand in me socks?   (He takes a practice swing on one side of the ball.)

MARY   No, bring me to a dump like this on our anniversary. (She sits on the bed and pokes it mistrustfully.)

CHRIS   (looking vaguely round)   Oh, it's not so bad. Decent golf course.   (He addresses the ball.) Fore!   (And he hits the ball out into the auditorium. It is, of course, celluloid. He puts the club back.)

MARY   Hmph! You and your golf.   (She knocks on the right side of the bed which produces an ominous hollow sound. She reaches over to the other side which seems reasonably springy.)   Well, bags I sleep on the left.

(She puts her handbag on bed, moves the cases onto the floor R. of bed and swings her feet over onto the left side. CHRISTOPHER opens the cupboard door D.R. and exposes a very large and decorative nude pin-up pasted on the inside of the door. He appears not to notice it and proceeds to stuff his haversack and fishing rod inside.)

CHRIS   But you always sleep on the right. Otherwise you have funny dreams, remember?

MARY   (bouncing up and down a few times)   Well, I could do with a good laugh. I need something to cheer me up after all I've been through.   (She lies down at full length.)

CHRIS   Oh, we're not going back to that again, are we?

MARY   Who was she?

CHRIS   Who?

MARY   The girl we met at the gate.

CHRIS   I've told you. She's one of the clients at work. (He puts his blazer round the golf-bag on the chair.)

MARY   She seemed to know you pretty well.

CHRIS   Just business.

MARY   So I noticed. I think it's time you stopped working at that theatrical agency. You're too exposed.

CHRIS   (anxiously)   Eh? Oh don't be ridiculous. They're
          just people looking for work. Most of them are very
          dull.

MARY   Like Miss Lamour or whatever she calls herself?

CHRIS   LaVerne actually – Bubbles LaVerne.

MARY   She would be a Bubbles.

CHRIS   (examining one of his golf-clubs)   I think I need a
          new driver.

MARY   (heaving up on one elbow)   You haven't worn out
          your old one yet. And don't change the subject. What
          is she – a chorus girl?

CHRIS   Good lord, no. Nothing like that. She's a stripper.
          (He puts the two tennis racquet handles up the blazer
          sleeves to look like arms.)

MARY   I might have known it. I suppose you leer at all your
          clients like that.

CHRIS   Yes – I mean, no. I've told you – I never look at other
          girls.   (He shuts the door D.R., double takes, opens
          it again, has a good look at the pin-up, shuts the door
          again hastily and stands with his back to it as though
          trying to stop her getting out.)

MARY   (sitting up)   It didn't look like it. Up she comes –
          all bosom and bangles – and rubs herself against you.

CHRIS   (shocked)   Oh here – look – I say – she didn't.

MARY   Yes she did. 'Allo, darleeng' she says –   (She
          puts on a pseudo-French voice and pout) –   'Fancy
          seeing you 'ere. 'Aving a naughty week-end?' I
          suppose that was for my benefit.

CHRIS   Oh, that's just her way. She's always like that.

MARY   I can imagine. And what did you do? Stood there
          grinning like a silly great ox and didn't even introduce
          me.

CHRIS   What good would that have done?

MARY   Then I could have snubbed her.

CHRIS   There you are, you see. I've saved you from yourself.
          (He drapes the car-rug over the bottom half of the golf-
          bag and down to the floor.)   Anyway, you wouldn't
          have liked her.

MARY   Liked her! I'd like to scratch her eyes out. She
         probably thinks I'm some bit of fluff you've picked up
         for a good time.

CHRIS   (soothingly)   Oh no, darling. No-one would ever
         mistake you for a bit of fluff.

         (This is really too much for MARY who throws the
         pillow at him.)

MARY   Oh! Oh! How could you? You beast!   (She bursts
         into tears and digs her handkerchief out from her
         handbag.)

CHRIS   Now what have I said?

MARY   (between sobs)   You don't love me any more.

         (CHRIS moves to the bed holding the pillow and tries
         unsuccessfully to embrace her.)

CHRIS   Yes, I do. Of course I do.

MARY   (shaking him off)   No, you don't. You like that
         Bubbles woman better than me.

CHRIS   Oh, blow Bubbles!

MARY   (in spite of herself)   What?

         (CHRIS stomps over to the armchair and stuffs the
         pillow under the blanket and blazer.)

CHRIS   Well, I mean, dash it. You're making a mountain out
         of a mole-hill.

MARY   Two mole-hills – and they're probably false. I still
         think it's funny her being here like that.

CHRIS   Yes, it was a bit of a surprise. I thought I'd fixed her
         up at Brighton.

MARY   Brighton!

CHRIS   In a show.

MARY   Nudes of 1968?

CHRIS   Maid of the Mountains actually.   (He puts his hat on
         top of the golf-bag with the badges to the front. The
         whole outfit looks like a slightly sinister stranger
         sitting in the chair.)

MARY   Ha! Anyway, you're not the only one with a secret.
         I've got a surprise for you too.

CHRIS   Oh goodie! I love surprises. What is it?

MARY   Wait and see. I'm not sure I'm speaking to you.

CHRIS   Oh, come on. Be a pal.

MARY   Promise you won't speak to her again while we're here?

CHRIS   (with actions)   See this wet, see this dry, cut my throat if I tell a lie. All right?

            (MARY nods and they kiss. CHRISTOPHER lowers her back on the bed and they are just getting comfortable when the main door opens and MRS. LOTT enters. She is an enthusiastic, rather large soul, determined to enjoy life and make sure everybody else does too - whether they want to or not. Smartly dressed, she indulges in large, over-ornate hats.)

MRS. LOTT   Ah! There you are, children!

            (CHRISTOPHER's feet shoot up in the air and the couple scramble into a sitting position.)

MARY   (patting her hair straight)   Hallo, mummy dear.

CHRIS   (astounded)   Mrs. Lott!

MRS. LOTT   Going to bed already? You must need a tonic, Christopher.

MARY   (moving to MRS. LOTT)   That's the last thing he needs.

CHRIS   But - but -   (To MARY) What's mummy dear doing here?

MARY   I told you I had a little surprise. Mummy and daddy are on holiday here too.

MRS. LOTT   Isn't it exciting?

CHRIS   Thrilling! You mean they're staying here?

MRS. LOTT   That's right, dear. We drove down this afternoon.

            (CHRISTOPHER falls flat on the bed.)

CHRIS   Oh no!

MRS. LOTT   Yes we did. I navigated. We only got lost three times - no. I tell a lie - it was four, because I said turn left when I meant right and we went into a farmyard. I told your father

he really mustn't take everything so literally.
But the farmer was very nice about it and showed
us round his new piggery. Actually the car was
in the middle of it but we managed to get it out by
borrowing his tractor. This is nice and roomy.

CHRIS   Yes, we were thinking of sub-letting.

MRS. LOTT   (peeping in the bathroom)   We're in the next
             block. Ours is the one with the sign on the door
             which says Ablutions. Your father said it used
             to be a dog-house. At least I think that's what
             he said. We each have a little compartment to
             ourselves. It's very cosy.

CHRIS   (sitting up)   That's a convenience.

MRS. LOTT   Oh yes. And it's so friendly. We get all kinds
             of people paying a call. They all seem to be in
             a tearing hurry and they don't stay long but it's
             nice of them to look in. One gave me a penny
             on the way out. I expect it's a local custom.

MARY   Wouldn't you like to sit down, mummy? You
             must be tired.

CHRIS   (R. of bed)   Yes, you need a holiday - no you
             don't - you need a quiet rest at home.

MRS. LOTT   (crossing U.R.)   Nonsense! We're here to
             enjoy ourselves. I said to Tom on the way down,
             'You're here to enjoy yourself so take that look
             off your face and settle down.'   (She looks out
             of the door.)   Where's he got to? Tom!

CHRIS   (hopefully)   Are you and Mr. Lott just here
             for the week-end?

MARY   No dear. They're staying for a fortnight.

             (CHRISTOPHER makes violently disapproving
             faces behind MRS. LOTT's back.)

CHRIS   That's all we needed -

             (MRS. LOTT turns round and CHRISTOPHER
             breaks into a ghastly smile.)

             - to make our holiday complete.

MRS. LOTT   Oh now, you mustn't take any notice of us. I
             said to Tom, 'They won't want to bother with
             us. We'll just mind our own business and let

them enjoy themselves!

CHRIS   Hear, hear!

MRS. LOTT   And do you know what he said? He said 'They'll
               be lucky.' Wasn't that nice of him?   (She
               looks out of the door again.)   Tom!   (To
               MARY.)   I expect he's stopped to light his pipe
               and lost his way. They all look alike, these
               huts.

CHRIS   Shallys.

MRS. LOTT   Yes, if you must.   (She inspects the number
               on the door.)   I thought you were supposed to
               be in Number Fourteen.

MARY   We are. There's a mix up over the numbers.
               (She sits on the chair L.C.)

MRS. LOTT   That's all right then. I was a bit worried when
               I saw Thirteen on the door.

CHRIS   Unlucky, I suppose.

MRS. LOTT   Don't be ridiculous. I'm not superstitious.
               (She moves D.R. and catches sight of the figure
               in the armchair.)   Ah! What's that?

CHRIS   Titfer.   (He picks his hat off the top and puts
               it on.)

MRS. LOTT   Thank heavens for that. I thought it was Tom
               for a moment. Now then.   (She claps her
               hands and CHRISTOPHER jumps.)   Come along.
               We mustn't waste time like this. Where are your
               trunks?

CHRIS   Eh? Oh!   (Pointing to cases.)   We only
               brought a couple of cases.

MRS. LOTT   No! Swimming trunks.

CHRIS   I don't think they'd fit you.

               (MRS. LOTT fixes him with a cold eye.)

MRS. LOTT   A good brisk swim will liven you up a bit.

MARY   Hear, hear!

               (CHRISTOPHER pushes the cases firmly under
               the bed.)

CHRIS   The tide's out!

MRS. LOTT	Then the walk will do you good.
CHRIS	But it's dark.
MRS. LOTT	That's all right. We'll stand on the sand and halloo you in. (She cups her hands and calls.) You are going on the rocks!

(CHRISTOPHER puts the golf-clubs, tennis racquets and rug in the cupboard D.R.)

CHRIS	I've just remembered - I forgot to pack my costume.
MRS. LOTT	Then it's just as well it is dark.
MARY	Come on, darling, don't be a coward.
MRS. LOTT	That's right. You'll both love it.
MARY	(startled) Both? (She jumps up.)
CHRIS	(chortling) Aha! (He shuts the cupboard door, puts on his blazer and moves casually L.)
MRS. LOTT	Yes, you're looking a bit peeky too. Your father and I used to love a midnight swim.
MARY	But -
MRS. LOTT	(dreamily) Floating there in the warm water gazing up at the stars -
CHRIS	Like a couple of rubber ducks.
MRS. LOTT	It was so romantic.
CHRIS	Here comes the decoy.

(The partner in the romance enters U.R. and rather destroys the illusion.   TOM LOTT is an untidy, shaggy man.   He seems to have a good deal of extra hair that he doesn't quite know what to do with and, although he is clean-shaven, he reminds one somehow of a friendly but rather moth-eaten St.Bernard dog.   He is dressed in ancient hairy plus-fours which look as though they smell of golf-balls and manure.   He is carrying a large golliwog and a bunch of seaweed.)

TOM	Looks like rain.

(CHRISTOPHER takes advantage of this diversion to slip unnoticed by the others into the washhouse, closing the door quietly behind him.)

MRS. LOTT	And where have you been?
TOM	Having a look round. Hallo, Mary love.
MARY	(kissing him) Hallo daddy. You're looking as enduring as ever.
TOM	That's because I get a lot of practice.
MRS. LOTT	(pointing to golliwog) What's that?
TOM	Seaweed. Oh this. I don't know. Chap handed it to me just now when I stuck my head inside the Palais de Danse. He said it was third prize for fancy dress.
MRS. LOTT	Never mind that now. You're just in time to hold the towels.
TOM	Who's fighting?
MRS. LOTT	No one. Mary and Christopher are going for a swim.
TOM	Ethel! You've been organising again.
MRS. LOTT	Now you know I never organise. I only suggest. (To MARY.) You're dying for a swim, aren't you, dear?
MARY	Well –
MRS. LOTT	There you are, you see. And so is Christopher – (She looks round vaguely.) Where's he gone? (She hoots loudly.) Christopher?
TOM	I expect he's gone to see if the water's warm. Now why don't you give Mary a conducted tour round our commodious quarters? (To MARY) We're lodged in the loo, you know.
MRS. LOTT	Oh, very well. Come along. It will save time tomorrow.
MARY	But what about Chris?
TOM	That's all right. I'll keep an eye open for him.
	(MARY picks up her handbag from the bed.)
MARY	Oh all right. But we mustn't be long because I know he wants an early night.
	(MRS. LOTT leads her to the door U.R. and across the window outside.)
MRS. LOTT	Nonsense! He spends far too much time in bed.

Why, when I was his age I was out on horse-back
every morning before breakfast. Now come
along and I'll show you the part they call the
Parade Ground. I'm not entirely sure what they
use it for but I've no doubt we shall be able to
get something organised before long –

(Her voice fades into the distance. TOM
watches them out of sight and comes D.C. shaking his head sadly. Then he goes to the bathroom door, changes the order of the letters to
read "N.O.C.", knocks on it gently, opens it a
crack and whispers in.)

TOM   It's all right. Coast's clear. You can come out
now.

(CHRISTOPHER's head appears followed by the
rest of him. He has put his sun-glasses back on
again and is wearing a towel under his sombrero.
He looks rather like an Arabian potentate.)

CHRIS   Has she gone?

TOM   Yes! Where did you leave your camel? Have a
prize.   (He gives CHRISTOPHER the golliwog.)

CHRIS   Oh thanks.   (He takes off his glasses and puts
them in his pocket.)   I thought I should have
to hide in there all night.

TOM   You can depend on your old dad-in-law. Now if
we look slippy we can have a quick noggin in
the NAAFI and be back here without them know-
ing.   (He hangs the seaweed over the bed so
that it dangles down just above the pillow.)

CHRIS   What about our things?

TOM   Oh, they'll be all right. Leave him on guard.

CHRIS   Eh?   (He realises he is carrying the golliwog
and throws it onto the bed.)   Oh lord! I would
have looked a right Charlie walking round with
that in my arms. Let's go out the back way
through the wash-'ouse.   (And he goes out
D.L., looking a right Charlie with the towel
still draped round his head and the badges on
his hat keeping watch behind. TOM makes a
deep obeisance at his back view and the chest/
lips and brow gesture of the true believer.)

TOM   Salaam aleikum, oh master.   (He follows
               after, shaking his head.)   I can see we're
               going to be a riot in the Bonanza bar.

               (The only sign of occupation left is the golly on
               the bed. Hardly are they out of sight than
               voices are heard U.R. and MRS. CURTAIN
               ushers in a tall, curvaceous blonde. MRS.
               CURTAIN has a fag dangling from her mouth
               and is carrying a small but expensive-looking
               suitcase. The blonde is very fashionably
               dressed and has a fur coat slung carelessly
               round her shoulders. MRS. CURTAIN shoul-
               ders open the door and peers at the number
               through a haze of cigarette smoke.)

MRS. C.   'Ere we are, love. Number Thirteen. This is
               your little Peedy Tare.   (She comes D.C.,
               puts down the case, folds her arms and pre-
               pares for conversation.)   Not too bad, is it?

BLONDE   (with an attractive French accent)   Eet is,
               'ow you say, sparse.   (She moves D.R.)

MRS. C.   Yes. That's the best of not 'aving too much
               furniture. It don't get too untidy.   (She
               crosses D.L.)   All mod cons through 'ere.
               (She returns to the bed and starts to buff it up.)
               Come far, 'ave you?

BLONDE   From Brighton.

MRS. C.   Oh! Right busman's 'oliday you're on then.

BLONDE   No, I came by train.

               (She drapes her coat carelessly over chair L.
               of door. MRS. CURTAIN picks up the golliwog.)

MRS. C.   Now 'ow did that get in 'ere? Sorry we 'ad
               such a business finding the right 'ut but it ain't
               really my job you know – ushing.

BLONDE   Ushing?

MRS. C.   You know, ushing people into their 'uts. I'm
               Mrs. Curtain. In charge of Entertainments.

BLONDE   Ah! I am in ze entertainment business too.

MRS. C.   Oh, well then. We're sisters under the pinny,
               as you might say. What line are you in?

               (The blonde opens her suitcase on the bed and

takes out a nightdress and a woman's magazine.)

BLONDE	I am an artiste.
MRS. C.	Drawring, eh? That's nice.
BLONDE	No, dancing.
MRS. C.	Oh! Ballroom or ballet?
BLONDE	Belly. Wiz bubbles.
MRS. C.	Get away. You're pulling my leg.
BLONDE	No, really, ees true. I am Bubbles LaVerne. (She quotes proudly.) Artistic poses wiz bubbles and fezzers.
MRS. C.	Fezzers?
BUBBLES	Hostrich fezzers.
MRS. C.	Cor! I'll bet they don't arf tickle yer fancy. Ain't that the cat's pyjamas!

(BUBBLES holds up her frilly, very short nightie.)

BUBBLES	No. Zis is my shortie nightie. Is chic, yes?
MRS. C.	Oh yes, very Arabian Nights. You know, I always fancied myself as a dancer when I was younger. But my hubby wouldn't 'ave it, not at any price.
BUBBLES	'E's a bit stiff and starchy, eh?
MRS. C.	I expect 'e is by now. 'E went off and left me three years ago. And by the time 'e'd gone I was past prancing round wearing a blush and a G-string. (She leans forward confidentially.) 'Ere! Let me into the secret. 'Ow do you stop them bubbles from bursting?
BUBBLES	Easy. We use detergent. It lasts the 'ole strip through.
MRS. C.	Well, if you're thinking of doing any re'earsing while you're 'ere, mind you don't bung up the drains with suds.
BUBBLES	Oh no! I am 'ere on 'oliday wiz Ernie 'Iggins.
MRS. C.	'Oliday? Sounds more like business to me – funny business. I thought you said your name was LaVerne.

BUBBLES	Ah! That is my stage name.
MRS. C.	A sort of 'nom de plumes', I suppose. Well, you could 'ardly call yourself Bubbles 'Iggins. Mind you, I don't mind a bit of 'anky-panky as long as people use their own 'anky. Where's Mr. 'Iggins now?
BUBBLES	'E's joining me 'ere tonight. (She sighs.) Eet 'as been a long time.
MRS. C.	Been away, 'as 'e? I never let Mr. Curtain out of my sight if I could 'elp it.
BUBBLES	'Oo?
MRS. C.	Mr. Curtain. My old man. Lovely, 'e was. 'E used to say, 'I may be a Curtain but I 'ave me frills.'
BUBBLES	'E's cute.
MRS. C.	What, my old man?
BUBBLES	(pointing at golliwog) No. 'im.
MRS. C.	You can 'ave 'im if you like. (She hands over the golliwog.) What's your bloke been doing, then?
BUBBLES	Time!
MRS. C.	Oh! Been inside 'as 'e? That's very 'ard on a girl, that is. 'As 'e been away long?
BUBBLES	Eighteen months.
MRS. C.	I don't wonder you took up bubble dancing. Takes your mind off things a bit. What did 'e do?
BUBBLES	They said 'e embezzled the camp funds.
MRS. C.	Oo! That was naughty. Was 'e in the Army?
BUBBLES	No, the NAAFI and 'e never embezzled a drop in 'is life. 'E was framed.
	(MRS. CURTAIN takes the pillow from the arm-chair and puts it back in position on the bed.)
MRS. C.	There's so many people in the nick who reckon they've been framed it must look like a blooming picture gallery. 'E'll feel at 'ome 'ere at any rate. It used to be an Army camp until last year.
BUBBLES	I know. This is where it all 'appened.

MRS. C.   What 'ere? Oh isn't that romantic. A rendeyvoo
on the scene of the crime. Brings back old times
I dare say.   (A thought strikes her.)   'Ere,
what became of the money 'e didn't steal?

BUBBLES   It never turned up.

MRS. C.   Oho! Makes you think, don't it?   (She goes to
the door U.R.)   Well, I mustn't 'ang about
'ere. I got things to do. I'm organdising a
knobbly knees contest. Think Mr. 'Iggins would
be interested?

BUBBLES   (tearfully)   I dunno. I can't remember what
'is knees look like.

MRS. C.   (putting her arm round BUBBLES' shoulders)
Oh that's 'eart-breaking, that is. Never mind,
dear, you'll soon be seeing them again. Mr.
Curtain used to 'ave lovely ones – all smooth
and shiny. That reminds me, I must let you
'ave your Bingo board.

BUBBLES   I don' play Beengo.

MRS. C.   'Course you do. Don't talk so silly. Everybody
plays Bingo. There's a board in every 'ut. And
the winner gets a special prize.

BUBBLES   I think I shall 'ave a bath.

MRS. C.   Oh no. You get what the organiser chooses.
That's me.

BUBBLES   But I don' want you. I want a bath.

MRS. C.   (soothing)   There, there. You're overwrought
at the thought of seeing 'is knees again. What
you need is a nice 'ot bath.   (She returns to
the door U.R.)   'Ere, you wouldn't like a job
on the camp, I suppose?

BUBBLES   I might.

MRS. C.   Rightyho love. We'll see what we can fix up.
Ta ta!   (She opens the door U.R., then
points at the Number Thirteen.)   You ain't
superstishus, I s'pose?

BUBBLES   Oh no. Mr. 'Iggins was most particular that
we 'ad Number Thirteen; 'e said it 'eld a lot
of 'appy memories for 'im.

MRS. C.   Per'aps he used to be a baker.

(BUBBLES doesn't react.)

MRS. C.   Baker's dozen.

BUBBLES   Doesn't what?   (She looks deliciously dumb.)

MRS. C.   Yes, well, never mind, love. I'll nip in a bit
later with your Bingo board. Don't forget to
wear your naughty nightie.

(She goes out U.R. closing the door. BUBBLES
puts the golliwog on the bed, spreads her nightie
beside it, unzips the back of her dress, picks up
her case and coat and goes out D.L. muttering.)

BUBBLES   Bakers does? Bakers doesn't?   (She closes
the door.)

(The lights dim to signify the passage of time.
As they come up we hear rather blurred voices
outside.)

CHRIS   (off)   I'm sure it's along here somewhere.
Eeny – meeny – miney – mo!   (He appears outside the window, followed by TOM.)   Here we
are. I'd know that puce eiderpane anywhere.

(TOM stumbles against the fire–bucket outside.)

Mind the fire–bucket.

TOM   Is that what it is? I thought it was a –

CHRIS   We don't wish to know that. Kindly henter the
'ut.

(TOM starts singing to himself.)

TOM   Won't you shilly in my shally, said the flider to
the spy –

CHRIS   Ssh!

TOM   (finger to lips)   Ssh!   (Cautiously they put
their heads round the door.)

CHRIS   (whispers)   Yoo hoo!

TOM   It's no good you yoo–hooing. There's nobody
home.

CHRIS   Then what are we whispering for?

(They enter. CHRISTOPHER carries his hat
and a towel rolled up as though returning from
a swim. He lays his hat down on the bed.)

TOM   We could have stopped and had another one.

CHRIS   Never mind, I've brought reinforcements. (He unwraps the towel and discloses a bottle of beer. He wraps it in his towel as though it was a baby in a shawl.)

TOM   Schnapps! (And he releases the leg of his plus-fours and produces a bottle of gin.) I usually keep my golf-balls up there. Got any glasses?

(CHRISTOPHER walks to the bathroom but stops with his hand on the handle.)

CHRIS   I expect there's a tooth-glass in the wash-house. (He is about to open the door but changes his mind and goes to the small cupboard L. of the bed instead.) Oh, no, wait a minute. Old Flannel-Foot said something about eating irons in here. With any luck – (He puts beer and towel on top of cupboard, gropes around inside and emerges with two large tin mugs.) Here we are. If you don't mind drinking out of jerry-cans.

TOM   More like jerrys. Still they'll do. (He blows them out and pours two slugs of gin into the mugs.) I thought you were going to have an early night.

CHRIS   Oh yes, so I was. Well, I can get ready for bed while we're waiting for the girls. Then I can't be sent off for a swim. Cheers! (He drinks.)

TOM   Good health! (He drinks.)

(CHRISTOPHER puts mug down on cupboard U.L., moves D.C. and starts to undress while TOM sits on the bed and starts to leaf through the magazine.)

CHRIS   Do you ever have the feeling you're being watched? (He suddenly turns his back.)

TOM   What's up with you?

CHRIS   (pointing at the poster) He's pointing at me. (He hangs his blazer over the poster and continues undressing.)

TOM   Ethel woke me up last night to tell me I'd stopped breathing. I lay awake for hours after that worrying.

CHRIS	What about – not breathing?
TOM	No – a bird.
CHRIS	I should have thought you were a bit past that sort of thing. What is she, a blonde?
TOM	No, a sporting fantail.
CHRIS	Sounds fascinating. (He pulls off his shirt and puts it on chair L.C.) I've never met one of those.
TOM	She's a bit broody.
CHRIS	Oh, bad luck.
TOM	I'm talking about my fancy.
CHRIS	So am I!
TOM	Pigeons.
CHRIS	Oh, them! Takes me all my time to stay on speaking terms with our budgie.
TOM	(pouring himself another drink) Fascinating creatures – pigeons. Did you know the Egyptians used them to foretell the future?
CHRIS	Omen pigeons, I suppose. (He is now in singlet and shorts and proceeds to do his evening exercises. These consist of isometrics – using the pull of one muscle against another. First he links his fingers in front of him and pulls mightily in each direction making twitching faces. Then he does the same thing with his hands behind him.)
TOM	(reading from the magazine) "Exercises for low-slung bottoms."! Good lord! (He looks at the cover of the magazine.) I thought this was Playboy. (He catches sight of CHRISTOPHER's antics.) Good God! What's up with you? (He hides the gin bottle behind him.)
CHRIS	Isometrics.
TOM	Is you? I didn't know you suffered from them. Better keep off the drink.
CHRIS	Special exercises. Tones you up. Jolly good for the old muscles. (He makes new faces, opening and closing his mouth like a fish.)

TOM   Looks more like indigestion to me.

                  (CHRISTOPHER lifts one knee and pushes down on it.)

CHRIS   There are some you can do with household gadgets.   (He falls over.)

TOM   I'd like to see you having a couple of rounds with the vacuum cleaner. My money would be on the cleaner.

                  (CHRISTOPHER goes to lean with his back braced against the door U.R.)

CHRIS   (panting)   You'd be surprised – the things you can do – with a broom handle.   (He bends forward, trying to touch his toes.)

TOM   I can imagine! Like the young man from Calcutta.

CHRIS   Ooh! This is a long stretch.

                  (The door U.R. bursts open, sending CHRISTOPHER sprawling. MRS. CURTAIN enters with a large board on which is pinned a Bingo card with a pencil on a string. TOM stands L. of bed.)

MRS. C.   (shouting)   Legs eleven! Oops! Sorry! Did you 'urt yourself?

CHRIS   No. Just upset my equilibrium.   (He gets up.)

MRS. C.   Oo! Language! I didn't know you'd got 'ere yet. Anyway, you shouldn't go 'iding be'ind doors. It frightens people. What you been up to?

TOM   He was doing a long stretch.

MRS. C.   Oh yes, I 'eard about that.   (To CHRISTOPHER.) Your missus was telling me.

CHRIS   (surprised)   Was she? I didn't think she knew.

MRS. C.   'Course she knew. Poor girl's nearly at 'er wit's end you being away so long.

CHRIS   We were only having a quick one in – Ow!

                  (TOM nudges him in the ribs.)

TOM   That's all right. I was keeping an eye on him.

MRS. C.   'Oo's this then, your Probation Officer?

CHRIS   He's Mr. Lott.

(TOM gives a little bow.)

MRS. C.   Has he? I'm not surprised, wearing them funny
           clothes.

CHRIS   No, but look here. What's my wife upset about?

MRS. C.   Well, it's your knees, you see.

           (CHRISTOPHER pulls up his shorts and examines
           them.)

CHRIS   My knees? What about my knees?   (To TOM.)
           What's she talking about?

MRS. C.   She misses 'em.   (Taking a look.) Although
           they're not much to write 'ome about. They
           might win the booby prize in a bad week.

CHRIS   (covering them up again and retreating D.R.)
           Do you mind?

TOM   Let's have another drink. Mrs. - er -

MRS. C.   Curtain. Me best friends call me Lacey. I
           don't mind if I do. Oh, by the way. I've brought
           your Bingo board.

CHRIS   That's all we needed.

           (MRS. CURTAIN goes to the door U.R. and
           hangs the board on a hook on the inside. TOM
           pours two drinks and hands her one. He moves
           D.L.)

MRS. C.   There we are! Brightens the place up. You're
           doing all right. You've got Number One and
           Number Eleven already.   (She takes the mug.)
           Oh ta! Bottoms up!   (She drinks.)   That re-
           minds me. You want to try a drop of liniment on
           your equilibrium.   (She rubs her bottom.)
           It'll take out the bruise.   (She sits on the bed.)

CHRIS   Yes, well, I was just going to bed.

MRS. C.   I didn't suppose you was dressing for dinner.
           (She drinks the rest of her gin and looks expect-
           antly at TOM.)   Nice drop of mother's ruin,
           that is.

           (TOM pours more into her mug.)

           Ta very much!   (She drinks and looks round.)
           Where's she 'iding?

CHRIS   Who?

MRS. C.   Got more than one, 'ave you? Your missus, of
           course.

CHRIS   Oh, she's out looking round the camp.

MRS. C.   You're a funny lot, you are. She's out sight-
           seeing. You're in 'ere standing on your 'ead.
           I 'ate to think what old baggy breeches 'ere is
           up to.

CHRIS   Tom?

TOM   Just one of life's observers.

MRS. C.   Oh, you're a Peeping Tom, are you? Well, it's
           none of my business. Mr. Curtain used to say,
           "Keep your trap shut and your fingers crossed
           and you'll come to no 'arm. "   (She rises, puts
           her mug on the cupboard R. of bed, and crosses
           to the door U.R.)   I must go and see to the
           cocoa. It's nearly time for Lights Out.

CHRIS   Lights Out?

MRS. C.   Didn't they tell you? The curfew's at 'arf past
           nine. Everybody in their 'uts until morning.
           Thanks for the drink. Oh yes, and send for me
           if you 'ave trouble with the lead in your pencil.

CHRIS   I beg your pardon?

MRS. C.   (tapping the Bingo board)   Your pencil. And
           don't get sucking it 'cause it's one of them purple
           inedible ones. Ta ta!   (She goes out U.R.)

TOM   (sitting in chair L.C.)   The more I see of this
           place the more I wish we'd gone to stay at Tor-
           quay. Still, I suppose there's one comfort -
           Ethel might stop out after the curfew and get shot.

           (CHRISTOPHER has meanwhile crossed to the bed
           and has been inspecting the nightie.)

CHRIS   What's this?

TOM   I don't know. Isn't it yours?

CHRIS   Does it look like mine? It's a nightdress.

TOM   Oh, is it? I thought it was a pocket handker-
           chief.

CHRIS   You're a bit out of touch.

TOM   Well, Ethel always wears pyjamas. She looks

like a Russion weight-lifter in a track-suit.

CHRIS   I suppose it must be Mary's but I don't remember seeing it before.

TOM   I expect she bought it for the holiday. They do things like that, you know. If they didn't go in for such flimsy stuff it'd last a bit longer. I've had this suit for twenty years and it's as good as new.

CHRIS   I can't quite see Mary in a Harris Tweed nightie

TOM   (pointing to nightie)   You'll see her all right in that.

CHRIS   Ssh!

TOM   Now what?

CHRIS   I thought I heard water running.

TOM   I expect it's the tide coming in.

CHRIS   (pointing D.L.) What, out in the wash-'ouse? (He listens at the door D.L. and beats a hasty retreat.)   It's Mary. I can hear her out there. She must have come back while we were out. Quick, clear up the debris.   (He pops his bottle of beer and towel and the mugs into the bedside cupboard while TOM stands up and puts the gin back down his trouser leg. CHRISTO-PHER picks up his hat from the bed.)

TOM   Blimey! That's cold! I'd better beetle off back to the old ablutions.   (He goes to the door U.R.)   It's the first time I've ever spent the night in one of them. Perhaps they'll make me a Privy Councillor tomorrow. Be all right, will you?

CHRIS   Yes. Give my love to mother-in-law.

TOM   (turning up his eyes)   I shall be very tempted to pull the chain. Good-night.   (He goes out U.R. leaving CHRISTOPHER listening at the door D.L.)

CHRIS   (calling quietly)   Mary?   (He listens but hears nothing.)   Mary? Didn't know you were back. I'm just getting ready for bed.   (In his agitation he puts his hat back on, then backs away from the door and starts to search around.)

Pyjamas? Pyjamas? Where the devil are they?
I'm not sleeping in my vest again.   (He calls,
crossly this time.)   Mary? Where have you
hidden the cases? Oh, I know.

(He crosses D.R. and ferrets in the store-room,
which is big enough to get inside. The door D.L
opens and BUBBLES enters wearing only a bath-
towel and slippers and looking delectable. She
crosses to the bed and picks up her nightdress.
Then she notices the magazine and starts to read
it as she moves D.R. and pushes the cupboard
door shut with CHRISTOPHER inside. Then she
returns, still reading, to the wash-house and
shuts the door. As the door closes on her the
door D.R. opens cautiously and CHRISTOPHER's
head appears with his hat pushed well down over
his eyes. He raises it and looks round suspiciously but sees nothing amiss. He enters holding
one of the tennis racquets and tries swinging the
door once or twice to see if it shuts on its own.
It doesn't.)

Funny!

(He leaves it shut and goes up to the door U.R.
with his racquet at the ready and goes out cautiously. As he disappears BUBBLES re-enters
D.L. in her nightie with her fur coat over her
shoulders. She is carrying her case. She
considers a moment then takes her goods and
chattels to the cupboard D.R., opens the door,
smiles a welcome at the nude and squeezes inside. CHRISTOPHER re-enters U.R., shaking
his head, moves D.R. and shuts the cupboard
door with BUBBLES inside, crosses to the bed,
lays his racquet on it, pulls out one of the cases
from underneath and takes it D.L. where he
knocks again on the wash-house door.)

Mary?   (He scratches his head, tries the
handle, finds it unlocked and looks at the letters
on the door.)   N.O.C.? Oh – knock.   (He
does so and gets no response.)   Are you decent?   (He peers inside.)   Mary? That's
funny. I could have sworn I heard her inside.
(He shrugs.)   Oh well!

(He goes out D.L. with his case and closes the

door. At once the cupboard door D.R. opens
and BUBBLES looks out cautiously. She emerges with the second tennis racquet at the ready.)

BUBBLES   Mrs. Curtain? Is that you?

(She also tries the cupboard door just as
CHRISTOPHER has done, leaves it shut, and,
pulling her fur coat round her shoulders, creeps
to the door U.R. and goes out with racquet held
high. As she goes the door D.L. opens and
CHRISTOPHER re-enters, wearing his hat and
bright pink pyjama trousers. He is carrying
his pyjama jacket which he puts on as he sits
down on L. of the bed. He lands on the tennis
racquet and jumps up again.)   .

CHRIS   Ow! Who the devil put that there? I might have
chipped myself.   (He puts the racquet on the
floor L. of the bed and climbs in. He then climbs
out again and takes off his shoes. He snuggles
down under the sheets with a happy sigh but
finds himself face to face with the seaweed. He
reaches up and squeezes it. It squirts in his
eye.)   Ow! Looks like rain.

(He settles down, cuddling the golliwog, and
pulls the sheet over his head – hat and all.
BUBBLES re-enters U.R. and closes the door.
With her back to the bed, she puts her fur coat
on the chair by the bed and turns off the light.
We can still see rather dimly what is going on
in the hut because of the light streaming in
through the window on to the bed. BUBBLES
sits on the R. of the bed, kicks off her slippers,
lays the tennis racquet on the floor and climbs in.
There is an interesting moment's silence, then –)

CHRIS   (sleepily and muffled)   Darling, you smell gor-
geous.

BUBBLES   (giving a little scream)   Oh! Oh darleeng!
There you are. What a lovely surprise!
(There is a loud kissing noise.)

CHRIS   (enthusiastically)   I say! The sea air's doing
you good.

BUBBLES   (reproachfully)   You 'ave shaved off your
moustache.

CHRIS   Yes. – Eh? – Moustache? – What moustache?
       Are you all right? You feel sort of different.

BUBBLES (gives a little scream) Ooh! – Your 'ands are
       cold. (There is another short silence – then:)

CHRIS   }
       (together) Mary?
     }
BUBBLES)   Ernie?

       (Pandemonium breaks loose. BUBBLES screams
       and CHRISTOPHER shouts 'Help'. They both
       jump out of bed. CHRISTOPHER catches his
       feet in the sheet and falls on the floor still
       shouting. Each grabs a tennis racquet and
       MRS. LOTT switches on the light disclosing them
       standing like a couple of Wimbledon champions,
       one on either side of the bed, their racquets aloft.)

BUBBLES You!

MRS. LOTT (in the doorway) Oh I beg your pardon!
       (She goes out.)

CHRIS   I think we've lost the ball.

       (BUBBLES lowers her racquet and bursts out
       laughing.)

BUBBLES You – ha! ha! It's you!

       (She subsides onto the bed laughing, laying her
       racquet on the floor. CHRISTOPHER also starts
       to laugh and sits on his side of the bed, putting
       his racquet on the floor.)

       I – ha! ha! – I thought you were Ernie.

CHRIS   And I thought you were my wife! (He takes off
       his hat and fans himself with it.)

BUBBLES (coyly) So I noticed.

       (CHRISTOPHER jumps up in a state of shock.)

CHRIS   Oh I say! I really must apologise. I had no
       idea –

BUBBLES You were pulling my leg, eh?

CHRIS   Yes. Sorry about that.

BUBBLES Don't be silly. (She pats the bed.) Sit
       down again, and tell me 'ow you knew this was
       my 'ut, you naughty boy.

CHRIS   No, no. It's mine. I mean I recognise the bed-
                spread and the stove and everything and –
                (The penny finally drops.)   Who was that
                looked in just now? Oh my hat! Mother-in-law.
                Quick, you must go.

BUBBLES   Go? 'Ow can I go like this?

                (She pirouettes in front of him. He subsides on
                to the bed again and hides his eyes with his hat.)

CHRIS   Put your slippers on or something. Somebody
                might come in. Oh lord! Mary will be back in a
                minute.

                (BUBBLES bounces down on to the bed beside
                him, showing a great deal of leg. CHRISTOPHER
                jumps up like a jack-in-the box.)

BUBBLES   So we tell 'er there 'as been a mistake, yes?

CHRIS   She'll never believe me. Look, Miss LaVerne –

BUBBLES   Bubbles.

CHRIS   Oh, all right, Bubbles then. This has put me
                in an impossible position.

BUBBLES   I think it was rather nice.   (She pats the bed
                again.)   Come 'ere and don' be so shy, you
                funny boy.

CHRIS   Oh I say, really, this isn't the time or place to –

                (BUBBLES reverts unexpectedly to raucous
                Cockney.)

BUBBLES   Come 'ere and sit down, you soppy great ha' –
                porth or I'll scream me flipping 'ead orf!

                (CHRISTOPHER, duly astonished, sits on the
                bed and puts his hat back on.)

                (Back to normal.)   I did a one night stand at
                the Old Vic. That's better. Now we work some-
                thing out, eh?   (She takes his hand.)

CHRIS   (trying feebly to rise)   But –

                (BUBBLES takes a deep breath as if to scream,)

                All right, all right! But hurry!

BUBBLES   (feeling his forehead)   Poor boy. 'E's all 'ot
                and bothered.

CHRIS   (looking at her bare legs)   I'm not surprised.

BUBBLES   A leedle bit feverish.

CHRIS   (feeling his own forehead)   I say, do you think
            so?

BUBBLES   We loosen ze collar, eh?   (She starts to un-
            button his pyjama coat.)

CHRIS   (feeling his own pulse)   I expect it's my holiday
            cold coming on. I usually get one about now.
            Here, I say –   (BUBBLES puts her hand inside
            his jacket and starts to stroke his chest.)

            Ha ha! Stop it! I think I'm going to sneeze.

BUBBLES   Press your finger under your nose.

            (CHRISTOPHER does so. BUBBLES eases him
            back on to the pillow.)

CHRIS   I've been oberworking.

BUBBLES   There, there. It's all zose pretty girls worry-
            ing you to give them good jobs.

CHRIS   Yes. Id's a bid ob a grind. And Mbary id terr-
            ibly djealous, you doe.

BUBBLES   (stroking his forehead)   Poor little Chrissy
            Whissy. 'Is wife don't understand 'im.

CHRIS   (trying to sit up)   Oh, I wouldn't say dthat.

BUBBLES   Yes you would! Now relax –   (And she pushes
            him roughly back on to the pillow.)   And I'll
            stroke your 'ead, eh?

CHRIS   It is rather comforting.

            (He relaxes. A voice is heard outside. It's
            ERNIE HIGGINS come to claim his own.)

ERNIE   (off)   Bubbles? Bubbles? Where the 'ell are
            you?

            (BUBBLES rolls CHRISTOPHER unceremon-
            iously on to the floor.)

CHRIS   Oy!

BUBBLES   (jumping up)   It's Ernie!

            (CHRISTOPHER sits on the floor rubbing his
            equilibrium.)

CHRIS	What did you do that for?
BUBBLES	Quick! It's Mr. 'Iggins. 'Ide under the bed.
CHRIS	(looking under the bed) But it's all fluffy.
BUBBLES	Oh, don't be so fussy. 'Old your breath.
CHRIS	What about my cold?
BUBBLES	Don't be such a baby. Quick! (And she pushes him out of sight under the bed. She goes to the window and calls.) Yoohoo! Ernie! Over !ere. (She jumps into bed and pushes a tennis racquet under the bed.)
CHRIS	Oy!
BUBBLES	Ssh! (She arranges herself to look pretty.)
CHRIS	Aa tishoo!
BUBBLES	Bless you! (She thumps the bed.) Shut up! 'E's coming.

(ERNIE HIGGINS enters U.R. He is about 45, short, wiry, common and cocky. Dressed in a very loud suit, he wears a nasty little moustache under a pointed nose.)

Darleeng!

(BUBBLES throws her arms wide, closes her eyes and pouts her lips for a kiss. ERNIE shuts the door and comes towards the bed but goes straight past and out into the wash-house. BUBBLES opens her eyes somewhat surprised to find herself alone again.

Hey! Speedy Gonzales! Where are you?

(CHRISTOPHER's head appears from under the bed.)

CHRIS	Under here.
BUBBLES	Get back.

(She pushes him back out of sight as ERNIE re-appears D.L. BUBBLES throws her arms wide again.)

Darleeng! You 'ave come back!

(But he takes no notice and strides across to peer into the cupboard D.R. Apparently satis-

fied at last he approaches the bed. By this time
BUBBLES is sitting with folded arms looking
grim.)

ERNIE   Wotcher mate! Glad to see us?   (He bends to
               kiss her and receives a fourpenny one across
               the ear.)   Oy! Wot's up with you then?

BUBBLES   That's just to remind you I'm 'ere.

ERNIE   I ain't likely to forget. I only wanted to make
               sure we was alone. Come on. Give us a kiss.

BUBBLES   Sure you wouldn't like to look under the bed?

ERNIE   (stooping)   That's an idea.

               (BUBBLES grabs him and drags him beside her.)

BUBBLES   Come 'ere.   (She wraps him in a voluminous
               embrace.)

ERNIE   Cor! Don't you smell soapy.

               (They go into a clinch with ERNIE on L. of bed.
               CHRISTOPHER emerges R. of bed and starts to
               creep off. He pulls the fur coat from the chair
               as he goes and covers himself with it as he creeps
               on all fours towards the door U.R. MRS. LOTT
               is heard outside. At once CHRISTOPHER freezes
               and pretends to be a mat.)

MRS. LOTT   (off)   I tell you they were playing tennis.

               (She appears outside the open window with MARY
               and they survey the huddle on the bed.)

               Oh look! Now they're playing squash.

MARY   Oh! I'll take his eye off the ball!   (She picks
               up the fire-bucket outside (which is preferably
               not too full!) and empties it over the two on the
               bed.)   How's that?

               (BUBBLES and ERNIE sit up screaming.)

BUBBLES)   Eek!

ERNIE   )   Ouch! 'Elp! Police! Fire! 'Elp!

               (MARY reaches in through the window and push-
               es the bucket down over his head. His cries
               take on an eerie metallic sound.)

MARY   Oh, shut up!

MRS. LOTT   Mary! Be careful, dear.   You'll dent it.

BUBBLES   (reverting to Cockney)   Blimey! I'm sopping
             wet. Let me out of this.

             (She leaps out of bed and lands on CHRISTO-
             PHER, who jumps up with a shout and runs for
             the cupboard D.R. still wrapped in BUBBLES'
             coat. She jumps back on to the bed.)

CHRIS   Ow! Help!

MARY   )
) Christopher!
MRS. LOTT   )

CHRIS   No. No. It's not me. I'm somebody else! I'm
             a polar bear!

             (And he shuts himself in the cupboard. ERNIE
             meanwhile has staggered off the bed and is bang-
             ing his bucketed head against the wall L.
             The door U.R. bursts open and MRS. CURTAIN
             appears ringing her large handbell.)

MRS. C.   Lights out! Lights out!

             BLACKOUT and QUICK CURTAIN.

ACT TWO

    Next morning very early.   The room is full of early morning
daylight which streams through the window.

                    When the Curtain rises it looks at first glance as
though the scene is the same as for Act One but
closer observation reveals slight variations.
The decor is identically drab, the curtains the
same, even the furniture is in much the same position; but the bedspread is bright yellow and the
pictures on the wall are different. Instead of
Kitchener we have Gordon at Khartoum, and Bude
in a fog has given way to a brown and fading photo-
graph of a Buffaloes Lodge re-union at Aldershot
in 1920. Later we shall see that even the nude in
the cupboard is different – if anything even barer
than the first. And when the main door U.R. is
opened we shall see that the number hanging on
the door is Fourteen.

                    Clearly this is Hut Number Thirteen next door.
A half-empty bottle of gin stands on cupboard R.
of bed. The room appears deserted except for
two humps under the blankets on the bed. The
hump on the Right is attached to a pair of large,
bare feet which stick out at the bottom of the bed.
Nothing is to be seen of the other occupant.

                    Suddenly the Tannoy over the door lets out a
yell.

TANNOY   Wakey! Wakey!

                    (This is followed by a loud Reveille on a bugle.
The owner of the feet falls out of bed and claws

himself upright. It's CHRISTOPHER still in
pyjamas. With his eyes tight shut he stands to
attention at the foot of the bed. The other sleep-
er doesn't stir. The Tannoy sounds Four Bells
and this is followed by an enthusiastic female
voice.)

Good morning, campers! It's six o'clock. Time
to rise and shine. Ready for your morning
exercises? Arms upwards – stretch! And –
down with a bounce and a bounce, stand up!
Down with a bounce and a bounce, stand up!

(CHRISTOPHER follows the instructions with
his eyes tightly closed but on the final 'Stand
up' he collapses on to the bed.)

Come along, come along. No slacking.

(CHRISTOPHER staggers back to his feet.)

That's better. Arms stretch, knees bend every
day keeps you regular, bright and gay. Now off
you go for a brisk run round the camp before
breakfast. Up – up – up – up – up – up – up –

(CHRISTOPHER does a knees-up run round in
a circle and climbs back into bed. The Tannoy
gives a final chime and subsides. CHRISTOPHER
embraces the figure beside him. The latter gives
a protesting snort and sits up revealing himself
as TOM wearing a deer-stalker hat.)

TOM   Oy!

CHRIS   (sitting up)   Eh? Oh, it's you!

TOM   Well, of course it's me. Who did you expect,
           Mary Poppins?

CHRIS   I'd forgotten about last night.

TOM   Well, I haven't. Running round in me smalls and
           swopping huts halfway through the night. – What's
           the time?   (Looking at his watch.) Good God-
           frey. It's only six o'clock. Go back to sleep.

           (They both lie down again. CHRISTOPHER sits
           up almost at once.)

CHRIS   I say!

TOM   What's the matter now? It's like being in bed
           with a blasted yo-yo!

CHRIS	Do you think she's all right?
TOM	Of course she's all right. That Higgins fellow will keep her warm.
CHRIS	Eh? No. I don't mean Bubbles. I mean Mary. It's the first time we've slept apart since we've been married.
TOM	(sitting up again) Now look, Romeo. Are we going to sit here discussing your marital habits or are we going to get another hour or two's shut eye?
CHRIS	She might be lonely.
TOM	That's the last thing she'll be. Sleeping with her mother is like sharing a hammock with a yeti.
CHRIS	But I miss her. You're not the same.
TOM	I'm glad you noticed. With Mary in her present mood you're better off with me – cold feet and all. Now pipe down.

(He disappears under the blankets again and CHRISTOPHER follows suit but sits up again almost immediately.)

CHRIS	(throwing back the clothes and holding his foot) Oh! Oh! Oh!
TOM	(sitting up yet again) Now what is it?
CHRIS	I've got cramp in my foot. Oh!
TOM	Oh, give me patience!
CHRIS	Ooh! Ow!

(TOM climbs out of bed and makes his way to the door D.L. He is dressed in a short nightshirt and his bare, hairy legs stick out below it. Round his middle he wears a black sash, judo-style.)

Where are you going?

TOM	I'm going to get a drink if you must know.
CHRIS	Will that do my cramp any good?
TOM	I don't know. But it'll do me good.

(He goes out D.L. CHRISTOPHER lies down

and pulls up the blanket.)

CHRIS   (calling)   Don't bother about me! I think I'm dying.

(At that moment the door U.R. bursts open and in comes MISS BOUNCE. She is a lady of about 35 - healthy, brimming with energy and fierce enough to frighten the pattern off the wallpaper. She wears an open-neck shirt, jodhpurs and riding-boots and her hair is pulled back in a tight bun. A whistle hangs round her neck on a string and she carries a riding crop which she wields like an officer's baton. When she speaks we recog-nise the voice on the Tannoy.)

MISS B.   (with a roar)   Stand by your beds!

(CHRISTOPHER peers over the edge of the blan-ket.)

What's this? What's this? Still in bed? Come on! Come on! Out! Out! Out!

(She smacks the bed with her riding crop and CHRISTOPHER jumps up and stands to attention on the bed, his cramp forgotten.)

We can't have slackers at the Sandpiper. When we say up we mean U - P - up!

CHRIS   But look here, I say -

(MISS BOUNCE smacks the bed near CHRISTO-PHER's toes.)

MISS B.   Quiet!

(He jumps in the air and lands at attention. She pokes him with her crop as though examining a lettuce for green-fly and moves L. of bed.)

Poor looking specimen. What's your name?

CHRIS   (snapping it out military style)   2375193 - Clifford C. - Sir!

MISS B.   What's the C for?

CHRIS   Swimming.

MISS B.   You're a fool. What are you?

CHRIS   I'm a fool, sir.

MISS B.   And don't call me 'Sir'. I'm Miss Bounce.

CHRIS	Yes, sir, Miss Pounce, sir.
MISS B.	Bounce! Bounce!
	(CHRISTOPHER starts to bounce up and down on the bed.)
	What's the matter with you?
CHRIS	I'm bouncing.
MISS B.	I can see I'm going to have trouble with you. Stop it!
	(CHRISTOPHER stops to attention.)
	I'm P.T.I.
CHRIS	I'm pretty high too. Can I get down?
MISS B.	Physical Training Instructor – I'm in charge of Gym.
CHRIS	Poor chap.
MISS B.	I turn shrimps like you into muscle-men.
CHRIS	I don't like shell-fish.
	(TOM re-enters D.L. with a tooth-glass and stands entranced behind MISS BOUNCE.)
MISS B.	That's got nothing to do with it. It does you good. Touch your toes.
	(CHRISTOPHER tries his best, still on the bed.)
CHRIS	I can't. I've got short arms.
MISS B.	Then turn up your toes.
	(CHRISTOPHER tries again. MISS BOUNCE takes a closer look. TOM coughs to convey his presence. MISS BOUNCE whirls round.)
	Great Heavens. It's Sherlock Holmes!
TOM	Good morning, my dear young lady. You're looking very trim and wholesome so early in the morning.
MISS B	(almost girlish) Oh, I say. Jolly decent of you to say so.
TOM	(pouring gin into his glass) Putting young Christopher through his paces?
MISS B.	As a matter of fact I was just inspecting his

short arms.

TOM	Hrrmph! Yes, quite. High time too. These young fellows need watching.
MISS B.	'Course they do. Always said so. Mr. – er –
TOM	Lott.
MISS B.	Sybil Bounce. How d'y'do? (She holds out her hand and they shake hands.)
TOM	How do.
MISS B.	(noticing his sash) I say, is that a black belt?
TOM	(casually) Yes, picked it up the other day.
MISS B.	I say! How absolutely ripping. Third Dan?
TOM	No. First Tom.
MISS B.	You must come and put me through my paces some time.
TOM	(doubtfully) Well – er – yes.
CHRIS	(still trying to touch his toes) Can I stand up now?

(MISS BOUNCE blows her whistle.)

MISS B.	'Tention!

(CHRISTOPHER stiffens to attention.)

Right! On the floor. Legs together, arms straight. Press-ups – begin. And one – and two – and –

(CHRISTOPHER scrambles down on to the floor across in front of the bed and starts to do saggy press-ups. The other two continue their conversation ignoring him.)

TOM	Bit early in the day to offer you a drink, I suppose.
MISS B.	Never touch the stuff .
TOM	You must get very thirsty.
MISS B.	Alcohol, I mean. Bad for the wind.
TOM	I get the same trouble with cucumber. Perhaps we could split a pint of milk some time.
MISS B.	Oh rather! Milk develops the pectorals. (She

breathes in deeply and expands her chest.)

TOM   So I see.

CHRIS   (collapsing on to his pectorals)   Help!

MISS B.   (poking him with her stick)   Now then. No
              slacking. And one – and two –

CHRIS   (puffing)   I – can't. I've got cramp again. It's
              agony.

MISS B.   Oh, we'll soon cure that.   (To TOM.) Take
              the other end.

              (She seizes CHRISTOPHER's feet. TOM puts
              his glass down on cupboard R. of bed and holds
              him under the arms.)

              Hey hup!

              (They swing him face downwards on to the bed
              with his head towards the door.)

CHRIS   No! Put me down! Help! I don't want to be
              cured. I like cramp! Ow!

MISS B.   Hold his arms.

              (TOM extends CHRISTOPHER's arms and holds
              them out straight. MISS BOUNCE kneels on the
              bed above CHRISTOPHER, pulls up his pyjama
              jacket and starts to pummel up and down his back
              with the sides of her hands.)

CHRIS   No! Ha ha! Oh! Stop it! Help! Tom! Eek! Get
              her off! Ow! I surrender. Oh! etc.

              (MRS. LOTT enters U.R. with a pile of TOM's
              clothes. She is fully dressed even to the floral
              hat. She stops, enchanted by the scene.)

MRS. LOTT   Ah! There you both are. Lying down again,
              Christopher?   (To MISS BOUNCE.)   Good
              morning, my dear. What a lovely morning.

              (She crosses L. and puts TOM's clothes on the
              chair L.C. MISS BOUNCE twists CHRISTO-
              PHER's legs into a figure four.)

MISS B.   'Morning.

CHRIS   Don't just stand there. Get her off. She's
              squashing my deltoids. Ooch! Grooch!

              (Because MISS BOUNCE pushes his face down

(into the bed and resumes her pummelling.)

MRS. LOTT   What dear?   (To MISS BOUNCE.)   I'm afraid he's not being very co-operative this morning. Never mind. You're doing a splendid job. Is it karate?

CHRIS   No, it's agony!

(TOM meanwhile has begun to creep off D.C. carrying his tooth-glass of gin.)

MISS B.   (turning CHRISTOPHER over and pounding his midriff)   He's got a flabby abdomen.

CHRIS   (gasping in time with the thumps)   And - a - thore - thorax - Ow!

MRS. LOTT   (to MISS BOUNCE)   I should think he's tender enough by now.   (To TOM.)   Tom! Where do you think you're going?

TOM   (retreating across R.)   Oh! Just - er - just going to have a wash, dear

MRS. LOTT   (pointing at glass)   You'll need more water than that.

(MISS BOUNCE releases CHRISTOPHER, who scuttles behind TOM for protection.)

Enjoy your little rub down, dear?

CHRIS   Rub down! She's nearly rubbed me out. I shall never be the same again.

TOM   Cured your cramp though.

CHRIS   I'd sooner have cramp.   (He clutches his back.) I think she's cockled me coccyx.   (He takes TOM's glass and drinks the contents, and bursts into a paroxysm of coughing.)   Good lord. That water's hard.

TOM   It was gin.

MISS B.   (advancing)   He needs patting on the back.

CHRIS   No, no. Keep her off!

(MISS BOUNCE snatches the glass from him.)

MISS B.   You young fellows need a bit more stamina.

CHRIS   I need embrocation.

MISS B.   (picking up her riding crop)   Now, don't forget

everybody. Cross-country run at eight o'clock
sharp. Twice round the perimeter.   (She
smacks her crop on the bed and everyone jumps.
To CHRISTOPHER.)   Including you.

CHRIS   Thanks very much.

              (MISS BOUNCE strides to the door U.R., which
              TOM opens for her.)

MISS B.   Thank you. Don't forget our little appointment
              with a pinta. And afterwards we can have a
              session on the mat in the Gym.   (She flips his
              black belt with her cane.)   Cheerio!   (She
              goes out U.R., taking the tooth-glass with her.)

MRS. LOTT   What was all that about Gym?

TOM   Nothing. We've been through all that once.

CHRIS   She thinks Tom's a ju-jitsu expert.

MRS. LOTT   I can't think why. He looks more like an Arab in
              that outfit.

CHRIS   It's his black belt.

MRS. LOTT   (inspecting it)   So that's where my black stock-
              ings went. Now then. What are we doing today?

TOM   Oh dear. Here we go.

MRS. LOTT   (to TOM)   You go and get dressed and stop com-
              plaining.   (She throws him his clothes.)   Here
              you are.

TOM   All right, all right. Anything for a quiet life.
              (He takes his clothes and goes to the wash-house
              door.)

CHRIS   Where's my gear?

MRS. LOTT   Gear, dear?

CHRIS   My clothes. I can't walk about like this all day.

MRS. LOTT   (appraising him)   Oh, I don't know. It's rather
              Carnaby Street. Suits you.

CHRIS   Please.

MRS. LOTT   Don't worry. I told Mary to bring your stuff
              over. And then we must be quick because it's
              such a lovely morning. The sun shining. The
              birds singing.

TOM   (lugubriously)   Those are owls.   (He goes out D.L.)

MRS. LOTT   The trouble with your father is he has no sense
of adventure. Oh no, he's not your father, is
he? Never mind.

CHRIS   I don't.

(MARY enters U.R. She is dressed in smart
slacks and a jumper but definitely lacks the holiday spirit. She carries a small fishing rod and
a sou'wester.)

MRS. LOTT   Ah! There you are, dear. You're just in time.
We're planning a really exciting day.

CHRIS   We're going hunting for owls.   (He goes to
kiss MARY.)   'Morning, darling.

(She thrusts the rod and sou'wester into his
hands and moves D.L.)

Oh, thanks. Just what I wanted.

MRS. LOTT   That's the way. You two can keep each other
company while I go and spy out the land.
(She goes to door U.R.)   I can't make my mind
up whether to enter you for water-polo or seven-
a-side Rugby. What are you best at, Christopher?

MARY   (grimly)   Indoor sports!

CHRIS   This is supposed to be a holiday.

MRS. LOTT   Of course it is, dear, but you must do something
to get rid of that tummy.

(She goes out U.R. CHRISTOPHER follows to
the door, patting his corporation and calling
after her.)

CHRIS   Solid muscle, that is. Ooh! I think that woman's
punctured my spare tyre.   (He winces with
pain. Closes the door and approaches MARY,
who is standing D.L. with her arms folded. He
takes a peck at the back of her neck but she
shrugs him off.)   Did you have a bad night?
(MARY says nothing. He tries to peer at her
face but she keeps her back turned away.)
I had a terrible time. Your father snores like
a porpoise.

MARY   Grampus.

CHRIS	I thought he was your father. Anyway, whatever sort of puss it was he kept me awake.
MARY	Don't you speak to me.
CHRIS	Now what have I done?
MARY	If you don't know, I'm not going to tell you.
CHRIS	Give me one good reason why I'm in the dog-house.
MARY	I won't. You'll only try to argue yourself out of it.
CHRIS	(stamping up and down) That's what I like about women. They're so damned logical.
MARY	That's right. Go on. Criticise! I suppose I'm the one who crept into the wrong bed.
CHRIS	All right, all right. I'm sorry. Now where are my clothes?
MARY	Where you left them – next door.
CHRIS	I thought you were bringing them.
MARY	Mother said bring your gear, so I did. (She points to the rod.)
CHRIS	Thank you. That was very thoughtful. What am I supposed to do? Stay in the hut all day or walk about like this? (He puts on the sou'wester.) Launch the lifeboat.
MARY	(moving to door U.R.) Do as you please. Why don't you go and get your own clothes?
CHRIS	(climbing on to the bed) How can I? That Ernie fellow is in there. I can see him moving about.
MARY	He'd be tickled pink to find you'd left your trousers in his wife's bedroom.
	(The Tannoy sounds 'Come to the Cookhouse Door.')
CHRIS	There. You see. Breakfast time. Now what am. I going to do?
MARY	How about catching yourself something?
CHRIS	Oh, very funny! I suppose you think I – hey, wait a minute, that's not a bad idea.

MARY   What?

CHRIS   Fish-hook.

MARY   Don't be rude.

CHRIS   No! Here, hold this.   (He gives MARY one end
            of the fishing rod to hold and starts to fit it to-
            gether.)   I told you last night you'd got hold
            of the wrong end of the stick.   (He reverses
            the part MARY is holding and gives it back to
            her.)

MARY   I suppose I dreamt it all.

CHRIS   No, it was all a little misunderstanding. I
            thought Bubbles was you, it's as simple as that.

MARY   How convenient.

CHRIS   Yes, wasn't it?   (He fixes the last piece of rod
            and pokes it out through the window towards the
            other hut.)   I knew you'd understand. Now
            then, if I can just get this in through the window
            next door and gaff my trousers.

MARY   Now you just listen to me.

CHRIS   Stand back.

MARY   Christopher!

CHRIS   Yes, yes. Just half a tick. Now then –

MARY   (stamping her foot)   Will you listen!

CHRIS   (steering with his tongue)   Ssh! I nearly had
            it that time. You jogged my elbow.

MARY   You're impossible. Do you hear? I'm going back
            to mother.   (She stamps U.R. and goes out.)

CHRIS   (without looking)   Yes, right ho. I think you'll
            find her on the Parade Ground.

MARY   (looking in through the window)   And take off
            that damned hat. You look like an advert for sar-
            dines.

            (CHRISTOPHER swings the rod and MARY ducks
            and disappears.)

CHRIS   Now then. Left a bit. Left – left. Got you!
            (He winds in fast and pulls in our old friend the
            golliwog.)   I must be using the wrong sort of
            bait.

(He unhooks golly and lays him on the bed. TOM
enters D.L., dressed and relatively decent.
CHRISTOPHER casts again. TOM watches with
interest.)

TOM   What are you up to?

CHRIS   I'm fishing for trousers.

TOM   Oh! Fly fishing, eh? Well, I suppose it makes
            a change from sticklebacks.

CHRIS   Ssh! I've nearly got something. Careful, care-
            ful. Got it!   (He strikes and there is a
            scream from outside. He pulls back, falls on
            to the bed and in sails the top half of a bikini on
            the hook.)

            You should have seen the one that got away.

TOM   (solemnly unhooking the prize)   I think you'd
            better throw it back. It's under size.

CHRIS   Half a tick. Somebody's coming. Look out!

            (He thrusts the rod into TOM's hand and hides
            L. of the bed. The door U.R. bursts open and
            MRS. CURTAIN comes roaring in.)

TOM   Oh lord! It's Old Mother Hubbard.

MRS. C.   'ere! What's going on? You got something of
            mine.

TOM   (holding up the bikini top) You must be joking.

            (MRS. CURTAIN pushes him aside and picks up
            the golly.)

MRS. C.   There 'e is. First prize.   (She snatches the
            rod from TOM.)   You want to watch what you're
            doing with that there winkle picker. You might
            catch more than you bargained for.   (She takes
            the rod apart as she speaks.)

TOM   We already did.

MRS. C.   You're nearly as big a nuisance as that feller
            next door.

TOM   Who, Ernie Higgins?

MRS. C.   That's 'im. Do you know what 'e did last
            night? Pulled up all 'is floor boards.

TOM   Perhaps he's digging an escape tunnel.

MRS. C.	And every time I go near 'im 'e 'ides in the bathroom.
TOM	I expect his best friends have told him.
MRS. C.	If you arsk me 'e's gone potty. That makes two of you.
TOM	Thanks very much.
MRS. C.	You can 'ave your toy back at the end of the 'oliday.
TOM	Yes miss.
MRS. C.	And I ain't a miss. I'm a missis.

(She goes out U.R. with the rod and golliwog. CHRISTOPHER bobs up. MRS. CURTAIN reappears. CHRISTOPHER bobs down again.)

MRS. C.	Oh, I forgot to tell yer. Two little ducks.
TOM	Eh?
MRS. C.	Twenty-two. On the blue.

(She goes out. TOM goes to the door and looks out.)

TOM	And twenty-two to you too. (He throws the bikini top at CHRISTOPHER.) Here you are, Isaak Walton. Don't forget your tiddlers. Sorry about the rod.
CHRIS	That's all right. It was the one you lent me.
TOM	Eh? (He rushes out U.R. shouting.) Hey! Mrs. Thing. Come back with that fishing rod.
CHRIS	(following to the door) Wait a minute! What about my trousers? - Tom! - Oh blast! (He returns disconsolate, shuts the door and holds up the bikini top.) Two little ducks.

(He marks off twenty-two on the Bingo board with the pencil on the string. Slowly the door opens and he retreats behind it until he is hidden. BUBBLES' head appears round the door-post. The rest of her is hidden.)

BUBBLES	Chreestopher? - Are you there? - Can I 'ave my top 'alf back, please?

(CHRISTOPHER's arm appears round the door holding the bikini.)

Oh, there you are.   (She steps into full view, dressed warmly in ski-pants and a roll-neck sweater. She carries a bundle of CHRISTO-PHER's clothes. She takes the bikini from his outstretched hand.)   Merci.   (She pushes the door shut, revealing CHRISTOPHER still in his sou'wester and pyjamas with one hand across his eyes.)

CHRIS   Mercy.

BUBBLES   Don't be shy. You can come out now. I can bear it.

CHRIS   That's what I'm afraid of!

BUBBLES   Silly boy. I am quite inspectable.

(CHRISTOPHER opens one eye cautiously.)

CHRIS   So you are. You had me worried for a minute. You haven't got any spare feathers, I suppose? I'm getting a bit chilly like this.

BUBBLES   (holding out his clothes)   Catch!

(CHRISTOPHER catches the bundle and kisses it.)

CHRIS   Thank heavens! I thought I should never see them again. You're an angel. Excuse me. It's a bit early for an audition.

(He stands the screen in front of the stove and scurries behind it. In the process he drops his trousers. BUBBLES picks them up and inspects them.)

BUBBLES   I'm worried about Ernie.   (She sits on the bed still holding the trousers.)

CHRIS   (peering over the top of the screen)   So am I! Do you think he'd recognise me?

BUBBLES   I don' think so. 'E 'as been acting very funny.

CHRIS   I'm glad somebody has.   (He throws his pyjama top over the top of the screen in the style of strippers in a dressing room.)

BUBBLES   'E spent all last night digging 'oles under the floor and muttering about finding something.

CHRIS   (pulling on his shirt)   Perhaps he's building a nest. I shouldn't worry. I expect he'll settle

	down in a bit. (His pyjama trousers appear over the screen.) Like to chuck over my trousers?
	(But before BUBBLES can oblige ERNIE's voice is heard outside.)
ERNIE	(off) Bubbles? Where are you?
BUBBLES	It's Ernie! Quick, let me 'ide!
	(She darts behind the screen. CHRISTOPHER pops out from the other side in his shirt-tails.)
CHRIS	Oy! What about me?
BUBBLES	'E won't recognise you like that.
CHRIS	Come on. Give me my pants.
BUBBLES	(throwing them over the top) Oh, 'ere!
	(She ducks down out of sight as ERNIE enters U.R. His head is bandaged and he wears a full-length rather snazzy dressing gown. CHRISTOPHER is hopping round on one leg with one foot in his trousers. ERNIE leaves the door wide open.)
ERNIE	'Allo, 'allo! Caught you on the 'op, eh?
CHRIS	She's not here.
ERNIE	(suspiciously) Who isn't?
CHRIS	Whoever it is you're after.
ERNIE	I'm not after anyone.
CHRIS	That's all right then. She just left.
ERNIE	I suppose you know what you're on about. (He stares round the room.) 'Ere! There's something fishy about this.
CHRIS	I expect it's the sea-weed.
	(ERNIE bends down to look under the bed.)
ERNIE	Cor! Me 'ead!
	(BUBBLES moves the screen across until it stands in front of the door U.R. CHRISTOPHER hops across to steady it and pushes her head down.)
CHRIS	Keep still! You're sticking out behind.
ERNIE	I usually do when I bend down. (He straightens

up and stamps D.R.)   Now then. Let's see what you're 'iding.

(CHRISTOPHER throws both arms out wide in front of the screen.)

CHRIS   Nothing!

(ERNIE throws open the cupboard door D.R., disclosing the very bare pin-up.)

ERNIE   Yes. I thought so. There she is.

(CHRISTOPHER peeps over the screen to re-assure himself.)

CHRIS   No, she isn't. She's still here.

ERNIE   (stroking the pin-up)   I'd know 'er a mile off. Recognise the eye-lashes. We used to call 'er Lulu in the old days.

CHRIS   You did?

ERNIE   This must be 'ut Thirteen. What are you doing 'ere?

(CHRISTOPHER is in fact still fighting to get his trousers on.)

CHRIS   Putting on my trousers.

ERNIE   I'm supposed to be in 'ut Thirteen. You're in the wrong 'ole, mate.

(CHRISTOPHER has been trying to get both feet into one trouser-leg.)

CHRIS   So I am. I knew there was something wrong. Thanks.   (He gets them on at last.)

(ERNIE notices that the screen has moved.)

ERNIE   'Ere! What's going on? That's moved. Are you 'iding somebody from me?

CHRIS   No, no. It's a poltergeist.

(ERNIE throws back the screen and exposes HORACE dressed as in Act One except that the cap has been replaced by a Robin Hood hat. He carries a large bow and wears a quiver of arrows. BUBBLES has made her escape unseen.)

ERNIE   So it is!

HORACE   (drawing his bow)   Stand on yer liver.

ERNIE	Cor, stone me! It's Eros. (He stands the screen R.)
HORACE	Do you mind?
ERNIE	I don't mind if you don't but William Tell would 'ave a fit.
HORACE	(proudly) I'm a toxhophilite, I am.
ERNIE	Are you? Well, you ought to be ashamed of yer-self.
HORACE	No, no. I'm in charge of harchery. Anybody want to draw a long-bow?
CHRIS	He's been doing that already.
ERNIE	(to CHRISTOPHER) Look here, Happy. Why don't you go and play 'opscotch or something?
CHRIS	No thanks. I've got one or two things to attend to in here –
	(ERNIE takes HORACE's bow and fits an arrow on to the string.)
	– Yes, well, as I was saying, I think I'll just meander down to the mess and have my break-fast. (He goes out hurriedly U.R. but looks in through the window and calls to HORACE.) Give my love to Maid Marian.
HORACE	You oughter 'ave a go with a bow. You might finish up with a quiver like mine. (He holds up his quiver with a shaky hand.)
ERNIE	That's what I'm afraid of. (He lays the bow and arrow on the bed and goes to inspect the number board on the door.) Now, look here, Robin Hood, I want you to do something for me.
HORACE	Ho yus?
ERNIE	I'm looking for a little black box about so big – (He demonstrates a shape about 2 ft. by 1ft.) One of me pals hid it for me in Hut Thirteen. Think I could swop over chalets without a lot of fuss? Then I can look for it quiet like.
HORACE	Ho nó. I never interferes with guests' partic-ulars. You'll 'ave to arsk Mrs. Curtain.
ERNIE	Not likely. I don't want that old scrubber inter-fering with my particulars.

HORACE	Well, I can't do nothing about it –
	(ERNIE holds up a £5 note.)
	– I'll go and get your stuff. (He snatches the note and stuffs it in his pocket.)
ERNIE	There's a good boy.
	(HORACE goes to pick up his bow from the bed. ERNIE goes to the door and takes off the number board. MRS. CURTAIN is heard outside.)
MRS. C.	(off) 'Orace! 'Orace! Where's 'e got to?
ERNIE	Oh cor blimey! It's Mrs. C. I'd know that fog-'orn anywhere. I'm just going to change.
	(He dodges behind the screen as MRS. CURTAIN enters U.R. carrying a golliwog. She stands, arms akimbo, where ERNIE was a minute before. HORACE turns round and finds himself face-to-face with her. He jumps.)
HORACE	Strewth! You did change, didn't you?
MRS. C.	What's the matter with you?
HORACE	Oh, it's you.
MRS. C.	'Oo did you think it was?
HORACE	I thought you was a werewolf for a minute. Where's 'e gone?
MRS. C.	Who?
HORACE	That 'Iggins feller. 'E was 'ere a minute ago.
MRS. C.	Never mind about 'im. You come and give me a 'and with a competition.
HORACE	Oh, not another one! What is it this time – Miss Fair, Fat and Fertile?
MRS. C.	No. I'm organising a treasure 'unt.
HORACE	You oughter 'ave a crutch and one leg. Long John Silver.
MRS. C.	I 'aven't got time for all them folderols. (She holds up the golliwog.) I've 'idden the winning number in 'ere. Now where shall I 'ide the golli-wog?
HORACE	'Ow about under the bed?

MRS. C.	No, that's the first place some of 'em look. I know – (She lifts the lid of the stove and pops the golliwog inside.) There. That'll keep 'em guessing. (She surveys HORACE closely.) You look like a refugee from the Archers.
HORACE	(posing D.L. with drawn bow) I'm one of the Merry Men.
MRS. C.	Well, why ain't you laughing?
	(The door D.L. is flung open and CHRISTOPHER bursts in to find himself face to face with HOR-ACE.)
CHRIS	Help! Oh, it's you. Excuse me! (He runs across past MRS. CURTAIN towards the door U.R.) Hallo, Mrs. Curtain. How are your pelmets? I'm trying to dodge mother-in-law. (He looks out of the door U.R. and jumps back again.) Oh, crikey! I'm surrounded. 'Scuse me! (He trots behind the screen D.R. There are various expostulations from behind it.)
ERNIE	(in a squeaky voice) Go away! I'm dressing.
CHRIS	What's going on?
ERNIE	Ssh!
CHRIS	Ssh yourself!
ERNIE	I was here first.
	(The screen sways perilously but doesn't fall.)
CHRIS	Look out!
	(Almost simultaneously MRS. LOTT enters D.L. and MARY enters U.R. At the sound of their voices the row behind the screen falls silent.)
MRS. C.	Uncle Tom Cobleigh and all.
MRS. LOTT	I'm sure I saw him come into the hut.
MARY	Well, he didn't get out this way. (She moves D.R. and looks in the cupboard, then joins the others D.L.)
MRS. LOTT	(to HORACE) Did you see anyone come past?
HORACE	Me lips is sealed.
MRS. C.	Like one of them brass monkeys.
HORACE	Do you mind!

MRS. LOTT   (to MRS. CURTAIN)   We wanted to enter Chris-
              topher for the Greasy Pole but he slipped through
              our fingers.   (To HORACE.)   Do let me hold
              your arquebus.

HORACE   (alarmed)   Eh? You keep orf. You 'aven't got
              a licence.

              (MRS. LOTT takes the bow and arrow from him
              and strikes a pose.)

MRS. LOTT   Oh, don't be silly. 'I shot an arrow into the air.'

MARY   Mother. Do be your age!

MRS. LOTT   Nonsense, dear.   (She lets loose an arrow,
              which has a rubber sucker. It hits the screen,
              which is hoisted up a few inches to expose two
              pair of feet and starts to edge warily towards the
              door U.R.)   Bulls-eye!

MARY   (pointing)   Look! There he is.

MRS. LOTT   (handing the bow back to HORACE)   He seems
              to have grown another pair of feet.

              (The screen comes to a halt but stays up in the
              air. MARY crosses and pulls it away.)

MARY   Now come on out and stop being childish.

              (She exposes CHRISTOPHER and ERNIE crouch-
              ing down. CHRISTOPHER has his eyes tightly
              shut. ERNIE is holding the Number Board in front
              of his face. MARY leans the screen against the
              R. wall.)

MRS. LOTT   Oh, look. He's found a playmate.   (She seizes
              ERNIE's free hand and pumps it up and down.)
              How do you do?

ERNIE   (still behind his board)   Go away!

MRS. LOTT   Now don't be unsociable. Come and be introduced.

MRS. C.   (going to ERNIE)   'Ere, that voice is familiar.
              'Aven't we met somewhere?

ERNIE   No.

MRS. C.   Funny, I could 'ave sworn.   (She suddenly
              snatches away the board, revealing ERNIE with
              CHRISTOPHER's sou'wester on back to front
              and well down over his face.)   Oh!

ERNIE   Keep 'er off!   (He pushes MRS. CURTAIN

aside and rushes out U.R.)

MRS. LOTT   (replacing the Number Board on door U.R.)
             He hasn't got the holiday spirit. That's his
             trouble.

MARY   Perhaps he's shy.

MRS. LOTT   Go and get him back, Christopher.

             (CHRISTOPHER, who has been standing all this
             time with his eyes shut tight, opens them and
             blinks.)

CHRIS   Eh?

MRS. LOTT   Fetch!

CHRIS   Oh! Rightho!   (He goes out hurriedly U.R.)

MRS. C.   Funny, I'm sure I know that feller.

MRS. LOTT   Yes. It's Christopher.

             (There is a crash from outside and cries of pain.)

CHRIS   (off)   Oh! Oh! Oh!

MARY   Now what's he done?

             (CHRISTOPHER reappears, hopping on one leg
             and clutching the other. BUBBLES is supporting
             him in a friendly way.)

MARY   What's the matter with you?

CHRIS   I've broken my ankle. Ooh! It's agony!

BUBBLES   (supporting him to the bed)   Poor boy. 'E fell
             over the fire bucket.

MARY   'E would.

MRS. LOTT   No wonder he looks a bit pale.

MRS. C.   I'm always telling 'Orace about them dratted buck-
             ets.   (She notices HORACE has dozed off and
             pokes him.)   Oy! Batman!

             (HORACE wakes confused and jumps to his feet.)

HORACE   What happened? Who won?

BUBBLES   (to CHRISTOPHER)   Let me 'elp you on to the
             bed.

MARY   (pulling her away)   Hands off! That's my job.

             (Unsupported, CHRISTOPHER falls flat on his

face on the bed. BUBBLES moves L. of bed.)

CHRIS	Ouch!
HORACE	What's 'e done?
MRS. C.	Kicked the bucket.
HORACE	(making for the door U.R.) 'Ere, I 'ope 'e 'asn't chipped me paint. (He goes outside and inspects his precious bucket.)
CHRIS	Never mind your rotten old bucket. What about me? Ooh! I'm crippled for life.

(BUBBLES turns him over on to his back and puts a soothing hand on his forehead.)

BUBBLES	There, there. Bubbles is 'ere.

(CHRISTOPHER holds her hand. MARY snatches his other hand on to her side of the bed.)

MARY	And I'm over here.
CHRIS	Ooch!

(MRS. LOTT moves to foot of bed.)

MRS. C.	Well, I can't stop 'ere being sociable. I'm arrang-ing a treasure 'unt. The winner gets an extra week's 'oliday free.

(CHRISTOPHER groans.)

CHRIS	Oh go away!
MRS. C.	What?
MRS. LOTT	I think he said Hooray! (She gets his shoe off and exposes a large hole in his sock.) Oh, Christopher! You've got a potato.
MRS. C.	Ah! Now that gives me an idea. 'Orace! (She goes out of the door U.R. and after a word or two to HORACE they both disappear off L. across the window.)
MARY	I've told him - I'm not darning his socks until he cuts his toe-nails.
CHRIS	What have my toe-nails got to do with it? What about my ankle?
MRS. LOTT	Lie still.
CHRIS	You're hurting.

MRS. LOTT   Don't be such a baby. I expect it's only a tiny
              fracture.

BUBBLES   Poor Christopher.   (She sits on the bed and
              strokes his forehead.)

MARY   Take your hands off my husband.

BUBBLES   You don' understand 'im.

MARY   Oh, don't I!

BUBBLES   'E needs comforting.

CHRIS   Yes, I do.

              (MARY yanks at his arm.)

              Ow! Careful. That's fixed this end.   (He tries
              to sit up.)

MARY   Lie still. I'm taking your pulse.

MRS. LOTT   (twisting his ankle about violently)   Does that
              hurt?

CHRIS   (shouts)   Agh! Yes, yes! It's agony.

MRS. LOTT   It's not numb at any rate. That's a good sign.

CHRIS   It's broken.

MRS. LOTT   Not a bit of it.   (And she tugs his leg into the
              air and wags it about.)   Look at that. Right
              as rain.

CHRIS   Ow!

MRS. LOTT   Hold him down, girls, while I get his sock off.

CHRIS   No, no! I haven't washed my feet. Ouch!

              (The two girls each pull their arm in opposite
              directions.)

MARY   Will you leave go!

BUBBLES   No!

MARY   He's mine, I tell you. Let go!!

BUBBLES   Let go yourself. You don' know 'ow to 'andle
              'im.

CHRIS   I feel like a wish-bone.

              (TOM saunters in U.R. with two table-tennis
              bats. He watches the two girls pulling in oppo-
              site directions and MRS. LOTT struggling with

CHRISTOPHER's foot.)

TOM   Anyone for ping-pong? Hallo, hallo! What's all
            this.

CHRIS   Help! Gerumoff!

TOM   You look like one of those saucy French post-
            cards. Getting pally in the shally. What's going
            on?

MARY   (pulling at one arm)   He's hurt –

BUBBLES   (tugging at the other arm)   – 'is ankle.

CHRIS   I surrender!

TOM   Well, if you could bear to put him down for a
            minute, ladies, I have an important message for
            you from Miss Thingummy – the one with the whip.

MRS. LOTT   Miss Bounce?   (She drops CHRISTOPHER's
            foot with a thump.)

CHRIS   Ow!

            (MARY and BUBBLES let go of CHRISTOPHER's
            arms and take notice.)

TOM   That's the one. Fine figure of a dragon. I've
            just been giving her the old back-hand slice in the
            Games Room.   (He demonstrates with a table-
            tennis bat.)

MRS. LOTT   Never mind that. What's the message?

TOM   Oh, yes. She's collecting all the ladies together
            in the grotto for a fashion show.

MARY   A fashion show?

TOM   Yes. Something to do with costumes. She said
            she'd meet you there in five minutes.

MRS. LOTT   We mustn't miss this, girls. Come along.

MARY   Where's the grotto?

TOM   It's the Nissen Hut with the papier mache rocks
            round the door and a strong smell of turps in-
            side. Used to be the paint store.

MRS. LOTT   Oh! What about him?

            (She points at CHRISTOPHER, who lies ex-
            hausted on the bed.)

TOM   Does he smell of turps too?

MARY	No - seaweed.
CHRIS	I'm dying.
MARY	Well, die quietly!
BUBBLES	Poor Christopher.
MARY	Oh, don't start that again!
MRS. LOTT	We can't leave him in this condition.
TOM	'Course you can. I'll look after him. I used to be a vet. Now buzz off and let the poor chap die in peace. Go on - shoo! (TOM shoos them to the door U.R. with his bats, like a man guiding aircraft on to a carrier. At the door MARY and BUBBLES bridle at one another. TOM pats them on the bottom.)
TOM	Oh, get on! Go and get blotto in the grotto! (MARY and BUBBLES go out U.R.)
MRS. LOTT	He needs a cold compress on his ankle.
TOM	I'll put a cold compress on you in a minute. Go away, woman.
MRS. LOTT	(at the door U.R.) And bind it up tightly. I do hope he'll be all right. Men are so heavy-handed. (She goes out U.R. and TOM closes the door after her. He takes out a hip flask. CHRISTOPHER sits up and stretches his arms out in front of him. One is about a foot longer than the other.)
TOM	That's better. Peace, perfect peace. What's the matter?
CHRIS	I've grown an extra foot on one arm.
TOM	Hmm! You'll be able to hire yourself out as a tripod. Treat for shock. Have a drop of moonshine. Do you good. (CHRISTOPHER takes a long swig while TOM looks in the bedside cupboard.) Where's the glass got to? (CHRISTOPHER wipes the back of his mouth and hands back the flask.)
CHRIS	Thanks! That Bounce woman pinched it. I expect there's another one out here.

(He jumps off the bed and goes swiftly to the bathroom D.L. TOM inspects the flask with interest.)

TOM   .   I've heard of miracle cures but this is ridiculous.
                     (Calling.)   Oy! What about your ankle?

CHRIS   (off)   What about it?

TOM   I thought you'd broken it or something.

CHRIS   (sticking his head in D.L.)   Ssh!

                     (He disappears again. TOM sits on L. of the bed
                     and takes a swig.)

TOM   I must try a drop of this. Might cure my dandruff.

                     (He inspects his hairy jacket closely. CHRISTO-
                     PHER reappears with a glass and a dusty black
                     tin cash-box about two feet by one foot.)

CHRIS   Here we are.

TOM   Would you mind telling me what you're up to?

CHRIS   Ssh! It's a secret.   (He looks out of the win-
                     dow. Whispers.)   Excused boots.

TOM   What?

CHRIS   Excused boots. It's the only way, don't you see?

TOM   If you ask me your feet have gone to your head.
                     (He pours a drink into the glass.)

CHRIS   Now look, everybody keeps pestering me to join
                     in and do things – right?   (He sits on R. of bed.)

TOM   Right.   (He takes a swig.)

CHRIS   Greasy poles, sack races. Heaven knows what.
                     I wonder I haven't been entered for the Beauty
                     Contest.

TOM   You might well win, judging by some of the talent
                     I've seen around. There's a girl working in the
                     Milk Bar with whiskers like a walrus.

CHRIS   It's the yoghurt – makes 'em grow like billyho.
                     Anyway, if I'm confined to me bed I can't go in
                     for any of it, can I?

TOM   (the light dawns)   Oh, I see. Old soldiers
                     never die, they only break their ankles.

CHRIS   Think of it. A whole fortnight in the pit with
                     everybody running round in circles – lovely!

(He stretches back on the bed and luxuriates.)

TOM   (pouring CHRISTOPHER a drink)   My boy. I used to think Mary had married a bit of a twit.

CHRIS   Thanks very much. I remember you said as much at the wedding.

TOM   I was wrong. You're a big twit. Cheers!   (He drinks.)

CHRIS   Bottoms up!   (He drinks.)   But why?

TOM   They'll never let you get away with it.   (He points at the black box.)   What have you got there – a medicine chest?

CHRIS   Oh, this? I found it tucked away in there behind the whatsit.

TOM   What's inside?

CHRIS   I don't know.   (He shakes it by his ear.) Bath salts, I expect.

TOM   Go on. Open it up.

(CHRISTOPHER stands, opens it and turns it upside down. Bank notes flutter in all directions. TOM springs to his feet.)

Blimey!   (He picks up a wad and riffles through them.)   Fivers! There must be a few thousand nicker. What a funny place to keep 'em. Hoy!

(Because CHRISTOPHER has snatched them from him and is shovelling them all out of sight under the sheets.)

There's no need to get greedy.

CHRIS   Ssh!   (He piles in more of the notes.)   I've just remembered.

TOM   What?

CHRIS   Mrs. Curtain's treasure hunt. This must be it.

TOM   Don't talk so daft. They give away second-hand tooth-brushes for prizes here.

CHRIS   (holding up a handful of notes)   I didn't suppose they were real.

TOM   Then what are you shoving them up your jumper for?

CHRIS	Because she said whoever wins gets an extra week's holiday free – and I couldn't stand it. We've got to find somewhere to hide it before she finds we've found it where she'd hidden it.
TOM	What?
CHRIS	I said we've got to find somewhere –
TOM	Yes, yes. All right! I see what you mean – I think. (He helps him stuff notes under the sheets.)
CHRIS	(ears pricking) Listen! Look out. Somebody's coming. Quick! (He jumps into the bed and pulls the sheet up round his ears.)
MRS. C.	(off) Come on. Don't take all day.
	(She enters U.R. with HORACE staggering behind. He is carrying a large pail of potatoes which he plonks down on the bed in front of CHRISTOPHER and collapses on to a chair D.R. wiping his brow with a large red spotted handkerchief.)
HORACE	It's bad for me back.
CHRIS	It hasn't done my shins a power of good either.
TOM	What is it?
MRS. C.	Spuds. They need peeling.
CHRIS	Oh no! The only peeling I'm doing is from sunbathing.
HORACE	They're King Edwards.
CHRIS	I don't care if they're Old King Cole's. I'm not peeling spuds on my holiday. Hey!
	(MRS. CURTAIN has whipped off the yellow bedspread and proceeds to pin it up across the open doorway U.R., leaving about three feet underneath.)
MRS. C.	(to TOM) Come on. Give us a hand.
	(He does.)
CHRIS	What's the idea? You don't have to keep me in isolation, you know. I've only hurt my ankle. I'm not infectious.
TOM	That's a matter of opinion!

MRS. C.	We're not having you lying around doing nothing on yer 'oliday. It's against regulations. So you can judge the competition while you're peeling potatoes.
CHRIS	(to TOM)　.Well, don't just stand there! You're a vet. Tell her I'm not fit for human consumption or something. I couldn't face a lot of knobbly knees.　(He lies back pale and wan.)
HORACE	'Tisn't knobbly knees. It's lovely legs. Smashing!　(He chortles and rubs his hands together.)

(MRS. CURTAIN glares at him and he subsides.) |
| MRS. C. | Be'ave yerself! |
| CHRIS | (coming back to life)　Oh well, that's different.

(He starts to get out of bed but TOM pushes him down again and hurriedly replaces the sheet.) |
TOM	Lie down. You're exposing your little treasure.
CHRIS	Eh?　(He looks under the sheet.)　Oh yes!
TOM	(to MRS. CURTAIN)　Perhaps I could help too. I rather pride myself as a judge of a well-shaped calf.
CHRIS	I told you he was a vet.

(MRS. CURTAIN calls under the bedspread.) |
| MRS. C. | Rightyho! Wheel 'em on!

(She takes up a position on the R. of the bedspread. TOM stands L. of the door.)

Quiet please. The first entry's just coming.

(A pair of very hairy legs comes into view beneath the bedspread.) |
CHRIS	You　must be joking.
TOM	Good lord. It's a horse!　(He bends down to take a closer look.)
MRS. C.	'Ere! What's going on? I'd know them knees anywhere.　(And she tears down the bedspread to reveal ERNIE HIGGINS dressed in a pair of swimming trunks and the sou'wester.)
TOM	It's hairy Mary from the dairy!

(ERNIE comes storming across to the bed, picks |

up the open cash-box and holds it aloft.)

ERNIE   Somebody's nicked me nickers!

TOM   I'm not surprised!

MRS. C.   (with a scream of joy)   Ernie!

ERNIE   (seeing her)   Winnie! Oh my gawd!   (He makes a dash for the door D.L. and goes out.)

MRS. C.   Stop 'im! Stop 'im! It's Ernie. It's Mr. Curtain! Me old man. 'E's come back. 'Elp! Oh!   (She starts to follow him, collapses into TOM's arms and they both fall on to the bed.)

TOM   Hey up!

CHRIS   Look out!   (He struggles out from under and stands on the bed, showering bank-notes and potatoes in all directions.)

           (MARY, BUBBLES AND MRS. LOTT - all wearing bathing costumes of appropriate seniority and degrees of exposure are driven in squealing through the door U.R. by MISS BOUNCE, who blows her whistle and wields her riding crop with cries of:)

MISS B.   One - two! One - two! One - two! Chest out! Bottom in! Get 'em up! Cut 'em out! Rawhide!

           (They run screaming across the room and out through the bathroom D.L.)

           CURTAIN

68

ACT THREE

> Late that evening. Outside it is growing dark but
> the light in the chalet is switched on. The puce
> bedspread and the pictures on the wall as for Act
> One indicate that we are back again in Hut 14
> (numbered 13, of course).

> On the bedside cupboard R. of bed a candlestick,
> matches and an enamel mug. On the floor L. of
> bed a tennis racquet. On the bed a dress and a
> scattering of female underclothing.

> When the Curtain rises the stage is empty but al-
> most at once MRS. LOTT passes across the window
> and peers in through the open door.

MRS. LOTT   Hallo?   (She knocks on the open door.)   Can I
come in?   (There is no answer and she tries
again.)   Are you at home, dear?   (She comes
further into the room. She is restored to normal
dress complete with flowery hat - if anything even
more flamboyant than in Act One.)

> (HORACE looks in through the window.)

Yoo hoo!

HORACE   (through the window)   Yoo hoo!

MRS. LOTT   (startled)   Who? Oh you! I thought for a moment
it was a sign of life. There doesn't seem to be anyone in.

HORACE   I expect they knew you was coming.

MRS. LOTT   Well, don't stand there like Sooty. Bring it in.

(HORACE leaves the window and reappears in the doorway U.R. He is dressed as for Act One, complete with muffler and whistle. He is wheeling a porter's truck bearing blankets and a partly inflated air-bed.)

MRS. LOTT   Oh, do stop looking so miserable. Whatever's the matter with you?

HORACE   Tain't right.

MRS. LOTT   What ain't – isn't?

HORACE   Three in a 'ut. It's against standing orders.

MRS. LOTT   That's all right. We shan't be standing. We shall be lying down.

HORACE   That's worse. That's committing a nuisance, that is. If they finds out I'll lose me licence.

MRS. LOTT   Dog or marriage? Put it down over there will you and blow it up.   (She indicates D.R.)

HORACE   Blow it up! 'Oo do you think I am – Guy Fawkes? (He tips the blankets etc. on to the floor and picks up the air-bed.)

(Meanwhile MRS. LOTT takes a look in the cupboard D.R.)

It's all go – go – go with you lot. I suppose you're part of that there jet set.

MRS. LOTT   Oh, no. We're all electric. I wouldn't have gas in the house.

(HORACE blows into the air-bed.)

HORACE   I'm not supposed to do this, you know. It confuses me lungs. You may not realise it, but under this 'ealthy exterior I'm not well.

MRS. LOTT   Laugh, clown, laugh.   (She moves U.L. and tries out the bed.)

HORACE   Eh?

MRS. LOTT   Pagliacci.

HORACE   No – fried onions. They give me wind.   (He has another blow at the bed.)

MRS. LOTT   Oh well, you're putting it to good use.

(MARY enters U.R., dressed in slacks and sweater.)

MARY	Hallo, mummy dear. I got your message. What is going on?
MRS. LOTT	Just a little re-organisation. I thought Miss LaVerne needed a little company to cheer her up. The poor girl's had a terrible shock.
HORACE	She's got another one coming.
MRS. LOTT	(ignoring the interruption) I mean, just imagine waking up one morning and finding you're a big-amist.
MARY	But she isn't. They're not really married.
MRS. LOTT	Well, whatever she is.
HORACE	Bigamistress.
MARY	That's more like it .
MRS. LOTT	You get on with your blowing.
HORACE	Only trying to be 'elpful.
MRS. LOTT	It's at times like this we girls must stick together.
	(HORACE makes a rude noise with his air-bed. MRS. LOTT fixes him with a stony stare.)
HORACE	Pardon.
MARY	She didn't seem unduly upset when I saw her.
MRS. LOTT	Ah! I expect she's numb with shock. Anyway, I've decided we must move in and help keep her pecker up.
HORACE	It ain't on the level.
MRS. LOTT	Isn't it? Never mind. We can't all have level peckers.
HORACE	No, this 'ere bed business – 'tisn't right.
MRS. LOTT	Well, blow it up more on one side then it won't notice.
	(HORACE shakes his head sadly and has a final blow.)
MARY	I don't think he approves of your plans.
MRS. LOTT	I don't see why not. Why should he mind if we all decide to spend the night together?
MARY	I can't say I'm madly keen on the idea either. Does he snore?

MRS. LOTT   Who dear?

(MARY points at HORACE's back.)

Oh, no! It's not him. It's you and me and Bubbles.

MARY   Oh, I see. You had me worried for a minute.
Well, at least I shall be able to keep an eye on
her.

(HORACE plonks the air-bed down on the floor
D.R.)

HORACE   There! That'syerlot.

MRS. LOTT   I thought it was onions. That was beautifully
blown anyway. Now all we need to do is make up
the blankets and sheets.

(She hands them to HORACE who mutters to himself and starts to make up a somewhat primitive
bed.)

HORACE   I ain't the chambermaid, you know. Work, work,
work! I dunno what some people think I'm 'ere
for.

MARY   By the way, does she know she's got company?

MRS. LOTT   What, dear? Oh, Bubbles, you mean. No, not yet.
But of course she'll be delighted when we tell her.

HORACE   (to himself)   Not arf she won't!

MRS. LOTT   I suppose we had better let the men know too or
they'll wonder where we've got to. They'll think
we've been kidnapped by white slavers.

HORACE   What about me?

MRS. LOTT   (looking at him doubtfully)   I don't think you'd
be quite right as a white slave.

MARY   More of a black sheep.

HORACE   That's right! 'Ave yer little joke. It's all right
for you. All fun and games. You don't care about
getting me into 'ot water, do you?   (To MRS.
LOTT.)   'Ow would you like to get stripped?

MRS. LOTT   I beg your pardon?

HORACE   That's what 'appens when a black-coat loses 'is
licence. They strips off 'is badges in the dining-
'all. Right in the middle of the prunes and custard.

MRS. LOTT   Oh, how messy!

HORACE   And Mrs. Curtain takes the pea out of 'is whistle.
             'Orrible it is.

MRS. LOTT   There, there. I'm sure you're quite safe.

MARY   Talking of stripping, where is 'you know who'?

             (MRS. LOTT goes to the bathroom door D.L. and
             stoops to listen.)

MRS. LOTT   I think she must be in here.

HORACE   She ain't likely to be in there.

MRS. LOTT   Yes, I can hear water. She's taking a bath.

HORACE   Blimey! It'll be the first one she's 'ad since she
             went to see the chirpyoperadist.

MARY   The what?

HORACE   The chirpyoperadist - the bloke what cuts her
             corns.

MRS. LOTT   He means chiropodist. The 'c's hard.

HORACE   So are 'er corns.

MRS. LOTT   I know just how she feels. But we must get on.
             Mary dear, would you mind slipping out and letting
             the men know where we are.

MARY   All right. If I can find them. The last time I saw
             them they were taking part in a Three-Legged
             Ladies Excuse Me.   (She goes out U.R.)

MRS. LOTT   I wonder where they find the three-legged ladies.

HORACE   (calling out of the window)   But keep it under
             yer 'at, otherwise we shall 'ave the Vice Squad
             round our ears.

MRS. LOTT   Vice Squad?

HORACE   Mrs. Curtain. She's vicious enough for anyone.
             Though what she's doing in the wash'ouse I can't
             imagine.

MRS. LOTT   Who said Mrs. Curtain was in the wash'ouse?

HORACE   You did.

MRS. LOTT   I said no such thing. You must have buzzing in
             the ears.   (She calls through the keyhole.)
             Hallo! Are you in there, dear?

BUBBLES	(off) Come in! The door's not locked.
	(MRS. LOTT opens the door and looks in.)
MRS. LOTT	Good gracious! (She shuts the door again quickly and turns to HORACE.) Shut your eyes.
	(HORACE does so and MRS. LOTT opens the door again and goes into the bathroom.)
	Whatever are you doing with all those bubbles – ? (She goes out and shuts the bathroom door.)
HORACE	(putting the finishing touches to the air-bed) Silly old article. I 'aven't 'ad buzzin' in me ears since I got a wasp in me 'at. I dunno why I put up with this place. Slog, slog, slog, morning to night. (He tries out the air-bed by bouncing up and down on it once or twice in a sitting position.) More than 'uman flesh can stand! (He swings up his feet and lays out flat.) Slavery. That's what it is. (He composes himself to rest.)
	(ERNIE peers round the door U.R.)
ERNIE	Pssst!
HORACE	(sitting up) Oh strewth! I've sprung a leak in me Lilo.
ERNIE	Oy!
HORACE	Oh, it's you, is it? They're after you.
ERNIE	(edging in) Is the coast clear? (He is disguised as a nurse, in cap and starched uniform and a wig. He carries a yellow bedspread, CHRISTOPHER's pyjamas and the Number board from next door.)
HORACE	Oh cor blimey! It's Florence Nightingale. Come and feel me pulse, it's repulsive.
ERNIE	Ssh!
HORACE	What are you all dressed up like that for – a secret operation?
ERNIE	No. I'm hiding. I found this lot in the First Aid Room. Do you think anyone will see through it?
HORACE	They won't arf get a surprise if they do. I thought you'd scarpered.
ERNIE	'Ow can I? I 'aven't found out where 'e's hidden the loot.

HORACE	I ought to turn you in.
ERNIE	What for?
HORACE	Desertion.
ERNIE	What, leaving Mrs. C.? That wasn't desertion, that was self-preservation.
HORACE	Yes, I see what you mean.
ERNIE	Good, then you can give me a 'and. (He starts to change over the Number boards on the door.) What we've got to do is make 'em think this is their shally.
HORACE	(moving U.R.) What good will that do?
ERNIE	Blimey! What 'ave you got between your ears, sawdust?
HORACE	No, me face.
ERNIE	(putting the old Number board on the chair L. of door) Well, I reckon that young fellow 'as 'idden the money somewhere in the other 'ut, see? So if we can get 'em out of it for a bit it'll leave the coast clear for me to 'ave a good poke round.
HORACE	But –
ERNIE	Oh, come on. Give us a hand. (He pulls the puce bedspread off the bed and starts to put on the yellow one. BUBBLES' garments fall on the floor.)
HORACE	'Ere! You mustn't do that. Firteen's yeller.
ERNIE	Not now it isn't. There! Lovely! Proper little yellow peril. (He spreads CHRISTOPHER's pyjamas out on top, picks up BUBBLES' bits and pieces and pops them in the cupboard D.R.)
HORACE	We shan't know whether we're in Chay Noose or Mon Reepoz.
ERNIE	No, and nor will they. Come on. (He makes for the door U.R. but retreats rapidly. He propels HORACE backwards on to the double bed.) Quick. Lie down on the bed.
HORACE	'ere, 'ere! What's all this then? Instant passion?
	(ERNIE sits him down on the bed and pulls a

stethoscope out of his apron pocket.)

ERNIE   Open your shirt.

HORACE   Blimey! The uniform's gone to 'is 'head. 'Elp!

             (ERNIE pushes him flat and opens his shirt.)

ERNIE   Lie down!·

             (HORACE gathers his muffler about him to def-
             end his honour.)

HORACE   'Ere! You're wrinkling me comforter.

ERNIE   I'll give you a once over.

HORACE   And I'll give you a fourpenny one in a minute.
             (He sits up.)

ERNIE   (pushing him flat)   Ssh! It's Mrs. C.

HORACE   I knew she wasn't in the wash'ouse. Blimey,
             that thing's cold!

             (MRS. CURTAIN appears at the door U.R. and
             glares round.)

ERNIE   'Evening!

MRS. C.   Droopy drawers.

ERNIE   What?

MRS. C.   All the fours. Forty-four.   (She ticks off the
             Bingo card behind the door.)   What are you up
             to?

ERNIE   (his back carefully turned and speaking falsetto)
             Check up.   (He sticks the stethoscope in his
             ears.)   Say ninety-nine.

HORACE   Eighty-two.

ERNIE   You're run down.

MRS. C.   Oy! Madame Curie.

HORACE   (into the end of the stethoscope)   You're wanted.

ERNIE   (rubbing his ears)   Ow!   (Falsetto.)
             Surgery 9.30 to 10.

MRS. C.   'Ave you seen a little runt about so 'igh?

             (ERNIE looks suitably disapproving towards the
             audience.)

HORACE	(sitting up) If you mean your 'usband – !
ERNIE	(interrupting him) Say Ah!
HORACE	Eh?
ERNIE	No – ah!
HORACE	Oh! Aah!

(ERNIE pops a thermometer into HORACE's mouth.)

MRS. C.	(coming D.C.) What's up with 'im, then? Twisted 'is braces?
ERNIE	(keeping his back to her) He's got acute inertia.
MRS. C.	'As 'e? I always thought 'e was an ugly old devil.
HORACE	(taking out the thermometer) Listen who's talking.

(ERNIE snatches the thermometer away and puts his hand over HORACE's mouth. He reads the thermometer, gives it a professional flip with one hand and pops it back into his apron pocket.)

ERNIE	One hundred and ten in the shade. I should advise total incontinence. Ow! (He shakes his other hand, which HORACE has bitten.) He bit me.
MRS. C.	I 'ope 'e isn't expecting rabies.
HORACE	So do I. I 'ate the little perishers.
MRS. C.	Not babies – rabies.
ERNIE	I shouldn't come too close if I was you.
MRS. C.	Is it infectuous?
ERNIE	No, but it's very catching.
HORACE	(sitting up) . Is it?
MRS. C.	'E looks a nasty colour to me.
HORACE	You don't look too 'ot yerself.

(MRS. CURTAIN begins to edge away but suddenly sees the air-bed.)

| MRS. C. | What's that doing in 'ere? It's supposed to be on the boating lake. |

HORACE	Boating lake! That's a good 'un. It used to be a static water tank.
	(MRS. CURTAIN at last manages to get a sight of ERNIE's face.)
MRS. C.	Half a minute! You're not the usual nurse.
	(ERNIE pops the thermometer into her mouth.)
ERNIE	No. I'm her brother.
	(MRS. CURTAIN takes it out again.)
MRS. C.	Brother?
ERNIE	Sister. (He snatches back the thermometer and puts it in his apron pocket.)
HORACE	Sister Hannah. 'E's left 'is banner outside.
	(MRS. CURTAIN spins ERNIE round and knocks his wig off.)
MRS. C.	Let's 'ave a proper look at you. Oh, my gawd! It's 'im! (And she faints into his arms.)
ERNIE	Oh, no! Not again! She must be anaemic. (He staggers back and they collapse on top of HORACE.)
HORACE	Get off! You're sittln' on me whistle.
ERNIE	Don't just lie there. Help me up. She's fainted.
	(HORACE struggles up and inspects his whistle.)
HORACE	Now look what you've done. You've punctured me pea.
	(ERNIE struggles up and dusts himself down.)
ERNIE	Never mind that. Lend me your scarf, quick.
	(HORACE unwraps his scarf and hands it over.)
HORACE	Feeling the draught, eh? It's them mini-skirts.
	(ERNIE starts to gag MRS. CURTAIN with it.)
	I often wondered why they calls them mufflers. I been longing to do that for years. What are you going to do with the body?
ERNIE	In the cupboard.
HORACE	She won't like that.

| ERNIE | (tying her hands with the stethoscope) She won't 'ave to. Give me half an hour and you won't see me for dust.   (He wraps her up in the puce bedspread.)   Come on. Give us a hand. |

(At this moment the bathroom door flies open and MRS. LOTT appears, looking back into the bathroom. ERNIE dives behind the screen and HORACE covers MRS. CURTAIN with blankets from the air-bed.)

MRS. LOTT   Well, you know best, dear, but it seems a funny place to rehearse. Don't stay in there all night. You'll catch your death. See you later.   (She shuts the door, turns and sees HORACE.)   Oh! You did make me jump.

HORACE   You didn't do me a power of good either.   (He makes a tremendous to-do with a spare blanket, using it to flap MRS. LOTT towards the door U.R.)

MRS. LOTT   My goodness. You are a busy little bee. I didn't think you had it in you.

HORACE   Ho yes. I'm a proper 'uman dynamo when I gets wound up.

MRS. LOTT   I thought you'd lost the key.   (She stoops down and picks up ERNIE's wig.)   What's this?

HORACE   I shouldn't touch that, if I were you. It ain't quite dead.

MRS. LOTT   (dropping it hurriedly)   Oh dear! Well, I shan't be long. I'm just popping down to the Pig and Whistle.

HORACE   'Ave one for me while you're there.

MRS. LOTT   (with dignity)   I am looking for Mrs. Curtain, if you must know.

HORACE   Ah, yes, well, I - er - I expect she'll be in bed. (He drapes another blanket over MRS. CURTAIN on the bed.)

MRS. LOTT   At this time of night?

HORACE   We all needs our beauty sleep.

MRS. LOTT   It doesn't seem to do some of us much good. You should try Horlicks.   (She goes out U.R.)

(HORACE sits on the bed exhausted. ERNIE emerges from behind the screen and puts his wig back on.)

ERNIE   That was close.   (He takes the blankets from MRS. CURTAIN and puts them back on the airbed.)   Look at 'er. Sleeping like a baby elephant. Grab the other end.   (He seizes one end of MRS. CURTAIN and HORACE takes the other.)

HORACE   I still don't see what's in it for me.

(They carry MRS. CURTAIN to the cupboard D.R., still draped in the puce bedspread.)

ERNIE   It's worth a hundred nicker if you keep your mouth shut.

HORACE   Are you offering me a bribe?

ERNIE   Yes.

HORACE   'Ow dare you! Make it two hundred.

ERNIE   Done!   (He pushes MRS. CURTAIN into the cupboard, slams the door shut and holds out his hand. HORACE spits into his own palm. ERNIE changes his mind and gives a scout's salute instead.) Nurses' honour. Come on.   (He makes for the door U.R. and picks up the Number Board from the chair L. of door.)   'Ere you are. Stick that up your jumper.

HORACE   Where are we going?   (He conceals the Number Board under his coat.)

ERNIE   Next door to dig for treasure.   (He goes out but comes back in again.)   Oh blimey! Somebody else coming. Anyone would think this was a 'oliday camp.   (He makes a dash for the bathroom D.L.)

(TOM and CHRISTOPHER are seen passing the window.)

HORACE   You can't go in there. It's full of Bubbles.

ERNIE   I don't mind.

HORACE   She might.

ERNIE   Quck then. 'Op on to the truck.

CHRIS   (off)   This isn't our chalet, is it?

TOM   (off)   'Course it is. Number Fourteen on the
             door. That's it.

HORACE   I ain't insured, you know.   (He climbs on to
             the porter's trolley.)

ERNIE   Never mind. I'm covered for third party risks.

             (He starts to wheel it towards the door U.R. as
             TOM and CHRISTOPHER enter. HORACE holds
             himself very stiff and straight. TOM is carrying
             a copy of Playboy. CHRISTOPHER is carrying
             a hot-water bottle. Both are dressed as in Act
             One.)

             (Falsetto.)   Gangway! Gangway please!   (He
             bends down and blows HORACE's whistle.)

TOM   Hallo!   What's up with him? Canteen food?

ERNIE   Elephantitus.

CHRIS   Elephantitus?

ERNIE   Yes. 'E's got trouble with 'is trunk. It's gone
             all stiff.

CHRIS   Poor chap.

ERNIE   I'm taking him to the theatre.

TOM   You should be just in time for the second house.

ERNIE   The operating theatre.

HORACE   (coming suddenly to life)   Oh no, you ain't!

             (He leaps off the trolley and disappears rapidly
             U.R. ERNIE chases after him with the trolley,
             shouting in his ordinary voice.)

ERNIE   Come back 'ere or I'll give you a jab with me
             hypowdermeric.   (He goes out U.R.)

TOM   Remind me not to report sick. I don't think I
             could stand the pace.

CHRIS   He made a quick recovery at any rate.   (He
             lays his hot-water bottle on L. of the double bed.)

TOM   Don't talk to me about quick recoveries. What
             about that ankle of yours?   (He transfers his
             pipe from his pocket to the R. bedside cupboard,
             peels off his jacket and loosens his tie. He hangs
             his jacket on chair R. of bed.)

CHRIS   Yes, I really put my foot in it there, didn't I?
            Are you sure this is the right hut? It feels diff-
            erent.

TOM   (pointing at the bedspread)   Of course it's the
            right one. Thirteen's yellow, remember? This
            is us all right.

CHRIS   (inspecting the air-bed)   What's this doing in
            here, then? I saw that last on the boating lake.

TOM   It's been pretty windy today.   (He throws
            CHRISTOPHER his pyjamas.)   Here - catch!
            These are yours.

CHRIS   How do you know they're mine?

TOM   'Cause no one in their right mind would be seen
            dead in them.   (He sits down on the double bed
            and removes his shoes.)   Let's get our heads
            down. It'll be lights out soon.

CHRIS   (taking off his jacket)   Where's your night-shirt?

            (TOM pulls the end of his night-shirt out from his
            plus-fours and lets it hang down over the top.)

            I thought you'd put on a bit of weight since tea-
            time.

            (TOM climbs into the double bed and sits in the
            centre.)

TOM   I'm ready for anything tonight.   (He pushes
            CHRISTOPHER's hot-water bottle down under
            the sheets by his feet, picks up his Playboy and
            starts to read it.)

CHRIS   (taking off his trousers)   Fine holiday this is.
            Spud-bashing half the day, two hours in the rain
            stuck up on top of the Big Wheel. I can't even
            enjoy lights-out at half-past nine sleeping in here
            with you. Very romantic, I must say.

            (TOM is engrossed in his book. CHRISTOPHER
            takes his clothes D.R. and opens the cupboard
            door, exposing MRS. CURTAIN wrapped in her
            bedspread. He doesn't notice her, of course,
            and throws his clothes inside and shuts the door
            again.)

            Mary won't even talk to me any more. She seems
            to think I'm doing it all on purpose.   (He picks

(up the enamel mug from the bedside cupboard and pokes round on the bed.) That's funny.

TOM That's me you're poking. What have you lost?

CHRIS My hot-water bottle.

TOM You don't need a hot-water bottle. It's supposed to be summer.

CHRIS But I'm thirsty.

TOM You can't drink out of your hot-water bottle.

CHRIS Yes, I can. It's full of coffee. I forgot to bring my thermos.

TOM (producing the bottle) Here you are.

CHRIS Thanks! I wonder how it got in there.

TOM I can't imagine.

(CHRISTOPHER unscrews the cap and pours some coffee into the mug.)

CHRIS Anyway, I don't see what Mary's got to be mad about. I gave her second prize in the lovely legs contest, didn't I?

TOM Yes, and you gave first prize to Bubbles.

CHRIS Well, I didn't want it to look like favouritism.

TOM You'll learn.

(CHRISTOPHER has re-stoppered the hot water-bottle. He sniffs his coffee.)

CHRIS This pongs a bit.

TOM What of – rubber?

CHRIS No. It's more like feet. Cheers. (He drinks.) Like a drop?

TOM (hurriedly) Not just now thanks. Might make me dream.

(CHRISTOPHER puts down the hot water-bottle and mug and climbs into his pyjamas. TOM pulls the bottle back under the clothes.)

CHRIS Think Mrs. C. will catch up with Ernie?

TOM Not if he can help it.

CHRIS (pulling back the blankets) Shift over then.

TOM   (pulling them back again) Not likely.

CHRIS   (tugging at them)   But you're bang in the middle.

         (TOM picks up the tennis racquet from L. of the
         bed and uses it to defend his position.)

TOM   That's right. And I'm stopping there too. You
         can have the life-raft.

CHRIS   Oh, come on. Don't be mingy.

TOM   I had enough of that mullarkey last night. Didn't
         sleep a wink.

CHRIS   But I don't like sleeping on my own.

         (TOM throws the tennis racquet at him.)

TOM   Then cuddle your tennis racquet and keep quiet.
         (He settles down.)   Good night. Don't forget
         to put out the light.

         (CHRISTOPHER sits disconsolately on the air-
         bed and removes his shoes.)

CHRIS   I feel like a ship-wrecked sailor.   (He toys
         with the racquet, considers a moment, then
         starts to use it like a paddle. After a few strokes
         he joins in, singing in rhythm.)

         Fifteen men on a dead man's chest.
         Yo ho ho! And a bottle of beer.
         Drink and the devil had done for the rest.
         Yo ho ho! and –

TOM   (sitting up)   Belay there!

CHRIS   (in his best Long John Silver accent)   Squall
         brewing on the larboard quarter, Jim lad. Make
         fast the 'atches, reeve up the fetlocks and shiver
         me timbers.

TOM   I'll reeve your fetlocks in a minute if you don't
         pipe down.

CHRIS   Ar!

         (TOM chucks a pillow at him.)

         Thank you kindly, zir.   (He touches his fet-
         lock respectfully.)   You wouldn't be 'aving a
         spare blanket as well, I suppose? It do blow a
         bit draughty round me main-mast.

TOM   No, I wouldn't.   (He lies down again.)

(CHRISTOPHER hoists himself to his feet.)

CHRIS   Ar! I believe I saw one in the locker, Jim lad.
             (He tries to use the tennis racquet as a miniature
             crutch and falls flat on his face.)

TOM   (sitting up again)   Now what's the matter?

CHRIS   The mice have been at me crutch.

TOM   Oh for Pete's sake put the light out and let me
             get some sleep!

             (CHRISTOPHER puts the racquet on the chair
             R.C., goes to the door U.R. and switches off
             the light. A mixture of moonlight and neon glare
             streams in through the window so that we can
             still see the action quite well.)

CHRIS   (in his normal voice)   You know your trouble,
             don't you?

TOM   Yes. I've got a twit for a son-in-law!

CHRIS   No. You don't breathe properly. Saps your en-
             ergy.   (He heads towards the cupboard D.R.)

TOM   If you don't let me get some shut-eye you won't
             breathe at all!

             (CHRISTOPHER opens the cupboard door. All
             is black within.)

CHRIS   Now then - blankets.

             (The door U.R. also opens and a shadowy figure
             looks in. It's MISS BOUNCE.)

MISS B.   (whispers)   Anyone at home?

CHRIS   (whispers)   There's nobody here but us vam-
             pires -

             (MISS BOUNCE turns the light on. CHRISTO-
             PHER sees who it is and shuts himself in the
             cupboard D.R. with a cry.)

             And I'm going back to my coffin!

TOM   (jumping up in bed)   Put that blasted light out!
             (Sees her.)   Oh my word!   (He takes refuge
             under the sheet.)

             (MISS BOUNCE shuts the door and comes to the
             bed. She is dressed in an attractive negligee

and her hair is flowing free. All things consid-
ered she looks quite a dish.)

MISS B.   It's no good hiding, I know you're in there, Mr.
           Lott.

TOM   (muffled)   I'm asleep.

           (She sits on R. of the bed and pulls down the
           sheet. TOM pulls it back up again.)

MISS B.   Tom? You haven't forgotten our little tete-a-
           tete, have you?

           (TOM's worried face appears over the sheet.)

           That's it. Don't be shy. You've nothing to worry
           about. We're all alone.

TOM   (looking round) No, we're not. There's, there's
           - dash it, where's he got to?

MISS B.   He's roosting in the cupboard. But we don't want
           him to hear us, do we?

TOM   Yes.

MISS B.   No, we don't. I want you all to myself.

TOM   Now look here. I - er - my dear young lady - I
           mean to say -

MISS B.   Call me Sybil.   (She holds out her hand as if
           to be kissed. TOM shakes it vigorously.)

TOM   How d'you do?

MISS B.   That's right. Now just lean back and make your-
           self comfortable. I'm going to let you into my
           little secret. Close your eyes.   (She starts to
           fish about inside her negligee.)

TOM   (takes a peep - closes his eyes tightly)   I say!
           Good lord!

MISS B.   All right. You can open them now.

TOM   (eyes tight shut)   No, thanks.

MISS B.   Come along, Thomas. Have a peep.

           (TOM takes a cautious peep.)

           Promise you won't tell?

TOM   Wouldn't dream of it.

MISS B.   (peering round suspiciously)   Well then – I'm
             Syd.

TOM   Who?

MISS B.   Syd.

TOM   Good gracious! What a marvellous disguise.

MISS B.   Nobody knows, of course.

TOM   They wouldn't, would they?   (He takes a closer
             look.)   Are you sure?

MISS B.   Oh, yes. I've been Syd for years.

TOM   Extraordinary! You ought to see a specialist.

             (MISS BOUNCE holds up a small card which she
             has produced from within her negligee.)

MISS B.   Do you want to see the proof?

TOM   (hurriedly)   No, thanks. I'll take your word
             for it.

MISS B.   (handing him the card)   Here you are.

TOM   (reading it)   Eh? C – I – D.?

MISS B   That's right, Syd.

TOM   Oh, Syd! I see! You know just for a moment I
             thought –

MISS B.   I'm on plain clothes duty. I think I'd better strip
             for action.

TOM   No, no. Please don't bother. You look better as
             you are.

MISS B.   Now, now. Business before pleasure.

             (She takes off her negligee and TOM hides his
             eyes again. He needn't have bothered, she is
             dressed as for Act Two. TOM sighs with relief.)

TOM   I think our policewomen are wonderful.

MISS B.   Well, now you've recovered from the shock – lis-
             ten. I want you to give me a hand.

TOM   Do I get a Deputy's Star?

MISS B.   No. But you can borrow my whistle if you like.

TOM   No, thanks.

MISS B.   Well now, this is what I want you to do –

(But they are interrupted by a shout from the cupboard D.R. and CHRISTOPER enters, his hair awry, and shuts the door behind him with a bang.)

CHRIS   Agh!

TOM   What on earth?   (He jumps out of bed.)

CHRIS   Somebody's left a deposit in the closet.

MISS B.   What?

CHRIS   There's a corpse in the cupboard.

             (MISS BOUNCE moves D.R.)

TOM   For goodness' sake! Whatever are you on about?

CHRIS   (pointing)   In there. It's all cold and clammy. It touched me.

TOM   You're touched, all right.

CHRIS   (hiding behind MISS BOUNCE)   Ssh! Listen.

             (They listen but hear nothing.)

TOM   I can't hear anything.

CHRIS   I told you – it's dead!

TOM   Oh, rubbish! It's the sea-weed. I hung it up in there to dry.   (He sits on the bed and pulls on his shoes.)   We haven't time to waste with fairy tales. We've got work to do.

CHRIS   (to TOM)   Talking of fairy tales. What's the dragon doing in here?

TOM   She's –   (He whispers in CHRISTOPHER's ear.)

MISS B.   Ssh!

TOM   You know who.

CHRIS   You mean – ?

TOM   Yes! Now shush!

             (MISS BOUNCE looks cautiously out of the door U.R. and gathers them round her.)

MISS B.   Gather round. I'm after this fellow – what's his name?

CHRIS   Horace?

MISS B.	No, no - Ernie.
TOM	Ernie Higgins?
MISS B.	That's him. I've been keeping an eye on him.
CHRIS	Poor devil.
MISS B.	(in an 'official' voice) We have reason to believe he has concealed some stolen money in the vicinity.
CHRIS	No. It wasn't in the vicinity, it was behind the – Ow! My toe!

(Because TOM has trodden on it.)

TOM	You mean to say it's real?
CHRIS	(nursing his toe) Of course it's real. What did you think it was – plasticine? (He wiggles it a bit to make sure.)
MISS B.	Oh, the money's real enough. The question is – what has he done with it?
TOM	Perhaps he's blewed it all on Bingo.

(MISS BOUNCE prowls round the room looking under and behind things.)

MISS B.	No. We think he's hidden it in Hut Thirteen.
TOM	In here?
CHRIS	Yes, don't you remember? It was behind the –
TOM	(to CHRISTOPHER) Ssh!
CHRIS	It was behind the –
TOM	Will you be quiet?

(CHRISTOPHER subsides and nurses his toe.)

MISS B.	What's he on about now?
TOM	Nothing. Take no notice. He's got a touch of damp rot.
MISS B.	Well, sooner or later he'll be back for the loot. So we're going to lay in wait and nab him.
CHRIS	Oh goodie! I always wanted to be an ambush.
TOM	You look more like a gorse bush.
MISS B.	(to TOM) You and I will scout round outside.

CHRIS	Don't forget your toggles.
MISS B.	(to CHRISTOPHER) You stop in here and hold the fort.
CHRIS	Hey! Half a minute –
TOM	(aside to CHRISTOPHER) What have you done with it?
CHRIS	What?
TOM	The money.
CHRIS	Oh that! I've hidden it in Hut Fourteen. But, look here, I don't want to –
TOM	Good lad! Keep it dark. (He tucks his night-shirt into his plus-fours and picks up his coat.)
CHRIS	You're not going to leave me on my own, are you?
TOM	You'll be all right. You've got the thing in the cupboard to keep you company.
CHRIS	But what do I do if he comes?
MISS B.	(heartily) Don't you worry. He won't get past us. But if you see anything suspicious – blow this and we'll come running. (She gives him her whistle and goes to the door U.R. followed by TOM.) You're much better off in here. He may be armed.
TOM	That's right. You stop in here out of mischief.
	(MISS BOUNCE turns off the light, leaving the room in semi-darkness.)
CHRIS	Oh no! Not in the dark.
MISS B.	He's not likely to come if we leave all the lights on, is he?
TOM	Besides, he can't shoot so straight in the dark.
	(They go out U.R. CHRISTOPHER creeps slow-ly D.C. Suddenly the door flies open again. CHRISTOPHER starts blowing his whistle like mad and hides under the air-bed. TOM switches on the light.)
	Forgot my pipe.
	(CHRISTOPHER emerges mopping his brow. TOM takes his pipe from the bedside cupboard,

turns off the light and goes out U.R.)

CHRIS   (chasing after him)   Don't you dare do that
again! Hey! Wait a minute! Tom! Come back!
Oh dash!   (He comes back in disconsolately
and shuts the door. He feels about on the bedside table.)   Where are those flaming matches?
- Ah! Here we are. Now then.   (He lights the
candle, puts the matches back on the bedside cupboard and creeps down to the cupboard door
D.R., carrying the candle. Eerie music plays
softly over the Tannoy. He knocks on the door.
(Falsetto)   Is there anyone there?   (He clears
his throat and tries again very deep.)   Is there
anyone there?   (Nothing happens. He laughs
nervously.)   There, you see. Nobody there!
(He sits down on the air-bed facing L., sets the
candle on the floor in front of him and puts on
his shoes.)

(Unseen by him as he chatters to keep his spirits
up the cupboard D.R. slowly opens and the shrou-
ded figure of MRS. CURTAIN emerges, shuffles
slowly across and stands behind him as he talks
away to himself.)

The 'Aunted 'Oliday Camp. What a recommend-
ation! Hot and cold running blood in every shally.
Roll up! Roll up! See the lovely lady. She takes
everything off - including her head! This way to
the 'orrible happarition. Now you see it, now
you don't. Half price children and old age pen-
sioners. Scare the pants off auntie for fourpence.
(He jumps up, side-steps round MRS. CURTAIN
and takes two steps D.R.)   Excuse me.
(He stops short and gulps. Then he notices
there are two shadows on the wall and only one
responds when he moves his arms and makes a
duck shadow. He calls softly.)   Tom?   (He
reaches behind him and touches MRS. CURTAIN's
bedspread. She groans loudly. CHRISTOPHER
yells.)   Tom!   (He dashes for the door U.R.
shouting and blowing his whistle. MRS. CUR-
TAIN follows him up and disappears behind the
screen.)   Tom! Miss Bounce! Syd! Help!
It's got me! It's the spook. It's the spook! It's
a puce spook!   (He rushes out U.R. shouting
and whistling.)

(As he goes the shadowy figure of ERNIE climbs
in through the window and hides under the blankets on the double bed. TOM and MISS BOUNCE
enter U.R. and TOM turns on the light. He looks
round.)

TOM   I can't see anything. What did you say it was?

(CHRISTOPHER peers in from behind MISS
BOUNCE.)

CHRIS   (breathless)   A spuce pook.

MISS B.   What?

CHRIS   I mean a spooce puke.

(TOM stalks into the room, blows out the candle
and restores it to the bedside cupboard.)

TOM   Nothing here.

CHRIS   Well, there was. It was ten feet tall with great
           glaring eyes. It must have come out of the cup-
           board.

(MISS BOUNCE goes to the cupboard D.R.,
throws open the door and shows it to be empty.)

MISS B.   See? Empty. Now pull yourself together.
           (To TOM.)   I've a good mind to arrest him for
           sounding his whistle after dark.   (To CHRIS-
           TOPHER.)   Give it me back. You're a dis-
           grace to the force.   (She snatches back her
           whistle from CHRISTOPHER.)   Ugh! He's
           wet my whistle.

TOM   (to CHRISTOPHER)   You know your trouble,
           don't you?

CHRIS   Yes, I'm a coward.

TOM   Then for Pete's sake get into bed, lie down and
           shut up.

CHRIS   Leave the light on then.

TOM   You wouldn't like me to read you a bed-time
           story, I suppose?

CHRIS   No, but you can tuck me in if you like.

TOM   Get out of it!

MISS B.   Oh, come along. We're wasting time. Let's

try next door.

(They go out U.R. CHRISTOPHER clambers into the double bed and immediately ERNIE sits up and pokes a gun at him. He is still wearing nurse's uniform, cap and wig.)

CHRIS   (screams)   Eeek!

ERNIE   Shurrup! They'll 'ear you.

CHRIS   (whispers)   Eek!

ERNIE   That's better. Now then, where is it?

(CHRISTOPHER points at the commode-like bed-side cupboard.)

No, no! Where 'ave you stowed the rhino?

CHRIS   You want the **menagerie**.

ERNIE   Are you trying to make a monkey out of me? Don't you understand plain English? I want to know what you've done with the brass - the lolly - the dough.   (In a cultured voice.)   Where have you hidden the money?

CHRIS   You mean where have I stashed the cash. Why didn't you say so?

ERNIE   Never mind the funny talk. Where is it?

CHRIS   I can't remember.

(ERNIE prods him with the gun.)

Ow! What big teeth you have, granny. Careful! That's sharp.

ERNIE   Well, you'd better look sharp too, 'cause I'm not fooling.

CHRIS   I hid it in the hut next door.

ERNIE   Where?

CHRIS   Up the flue.

ERNIE   What?

CHRIS   In the stove.

ERNIE   That's more like it. Now we're talking the same language.

CHRIS   I doubt it.

(ERNIE gets out of bed, revealing the nurse's uniform.)

I say! Kindly adjust your dress before leaving.

ERNIE   Come on - out.

CHRIS   I've only just got in.

ERNIE   (shouting)   OUT!

CHRIS   (climbing out of bed)   Ssh!

ERNIE   (whispers)   I'm taking you with me just to make sure you're not 'aving me on. Come on. Get cracking.   (He steers CHRISTOPHER at gun-point to the door U.R., switches off the light and peers out. He ducks back in again.)   Look out. They've spotted me. Quick, out the back.

(A whistle is blown outside and TOM and MISS BOUNCE can be heard shouting. ERNIE runs to the bathroom and opens the door.)

TOM   (off)   There he is, in the hut.

MISS B.   (off)   View tallyho!

(BUBBLES screams in the bathroom. ERNIE shuts the door.)

ERNIE   Oh blimey! Back into bed.   (He manhandles CHRISTOPHER back to the bed.)

CHRIS   Unhand me, madam. Help! I'm too young.

ERNIE   Shurrup!

(TOM and MISS BOUNCE burst in U.R. and switch on the light. They see the two on the bed trying to hide under the bedspread and sit on top of them. MARY enters U.R. and stands amazed.)

MISS B.   Sit on his head! Don't let him get away!

TOM   (bouncing up and down)   Down with a bounce and a bounce.

MARY   What on earth are you doing?

(There are muffled shouts from under the bed-spread and a good deal of thrashing about.)

MISS B.   We've got him.

TOM   Caught him in the act. Got him red-handed.

Look!   (He pulls back the bedspread and reveals CHRISTOPHER and ERNIE.)

MARY   You beast! You're at it again!

(She looks round and picks up CHRISTOPHER's
mug of coffee from bedside cupboard. CHRISTO-
PHER scrambles to the edge of the bed on hands
and knees.)

CHRIS   Now listen, Mary. I can explain –   (He ducks
his head under the clothes as MARY empties the
coffee over his back half.)   Argh! It's gone
cold!

(MARY bangs the mug on the bedside cupboard.)

MARY   Take that.

ERNIE   And that!   (He thumps CHRISTOPHER with the
pillow and goes out of the window.)

TOM   (to CHRISTOPHER)   You great twit! You let
him get away.

CHRIS   That wasn't a him. It was a her.

TOM   With those boots? It was Ernie.

CHRIS   I thought he was a funny shape.

MISS B.   After him!'   (She chases out through the door
U.R.)

(There are moans from behind the screen.)

CHRIS   What's that?

(TOM moves the screen aside and exposes MRS.
CURTAIN, still in her shroud.)

It's the monster from the lagoon! Keep it off!
(He takes refuge behind MARY.)

TOM   Good god! It's like the Mummy Room at the Brit-
ish Museum. I hereby declare this waxworks
well and truly open.   (He pulls off the bedspread and reveals MRS. CURTAIN bound and
gagged.)   Good lord!' It is the Mummy Room.

MARY   (running to help her)   Mrs. Curtain!   (To
TOM.)   Don't just stand there gaping. Untie
her.   (She unties the muffler as TOM sets to
work on the stethoscope.)

TOM	I expect it's a new party game. Hunt the Curtain.
MARY	Are you all right?
MRS. C.	Cor strewth! I 'aven't 'ad a night like this since we 'ad a block-buster in the basement. (She staggers over to the bed with MARY supporting her.) I've come over all 'owsyerfather.

(TOM takes out a hip flask and pours her a drink into the coffee mug.)

MARY.	Poor Mrs. Curtain
MISS B.	(looking in through the window) Treat for shock.
TOM	Here you are. Try a drop of this.
MRS. C.	(sniffing it suspiciously) What is it?
TOM	Shock absorber. Do you good.
MRS. C.	Ta! (She takes a drink.)
CHRIS	(sitting on L. of the bed) What about me?
MARY	You shut up and shift over.

(He does.)

Put your feet up, Mrs. Curtain. I'll light the stove and get a bit of heat going.

(She picks up the matches and goes to the stove. TOM helps MRS. CURTAIN to put her feet up on the bed, shoving CHRISTOPHER off on to the floor in the process.)

CHRIS	Oy!
MRS. C.	Mud in yer eye! (She drinks, then feels the bed.) The bed's a bit damp.
MARY	There's been a drip on it.
CHRIS	(clambering to his feet) Thanks very much. (He feels the seat of his pyjamas.)
MRS. C.	Where's Ernie?
MISS B.	(entering U. R. in time to hear this) Got away, I'm afraid. Not to worry. We'll get him in the end.
MRS. C.	That's just where I'd like to get 'im.

MARY   (to CHRISTOPHER)   Come on. Stop admiring
                yourself and make yourself useful; Find some
                paper.

                (CHRISTOPHER stops trying to inspect his
                trouser seat, looks round and seizes on TOM's
                Playboy magazine. He takes it to MARY.)

CHRIS   Here you are.

                (MARY proceeds to tear it up and stuff it in the
                stove.)

TOM   Hoy! That's my Playboy.

MARY   Should burn rather well.

CHRIS   (to TOM)   My trousers are soaked.

TOM   Well, take 'em off then and dry them by the fire.

CHRIS   What here? Not likely.

                (TOM indicates MISS BOUNCE, who is bending
                down investigating under the bed.)

TOM   Syd won't mind. He's very broad – er – minded.

                (CHRISTOPHER sits down on the stove to watch
                developments. MARY finishes lighting it and
                stands R. of main door.)

MRS. C.   (holding out her mug and pointing at MISS BOUNCE.
                What's she looking for – men?

TOM   (pouring her another drink)   She's hunting for
                treasure.

MRS. C.   Oh yes. I'd forgotten about the treasure hunt.
                (She looks towards CHRISTOPHER.)   One of
                you is getting very warm.

MARY   (sniffing) What's that smell of coffee?

TOM   It's Christopher. He's percolated himself.

MRS. C.   (waving her mug about)   Bottoms up!   (She
                drinks.)

                (CHRISTOPHER jumps off the stove with a shout,
                clutches his bottom and scurries behind the
                screen.)

CHRIS   Ow! That's hot!

                (The door U.R. bursts open and in comes ERNIE,

still in his nurse's uniform but without cap or wig
and with his head through a tennis racquet frame
which is steered at the handle end by MRS. LOTT.
In her free hand MRS. LOTT carries ERNIE's gun.
Under her arm is tucked a golliwog.)

MARY)	It's Mr. Higgins!
TOM)	Oh,, well bowled!
MISS B.)	Got him!
CHRIS)	Hooray!

(MRS. LOTT takes off the racquet. ERNIE
clutches at his ears.)

ERNIE   Mind me ears!

MRS. C.   (standing up)   Ernie!   (She stretches out her
arms, the mug discarded.)

(TOM manoeuvres himself into a position to catch
her.)

TOM   Here we go again!

(But ERNIE faints instead into a graceful heap.
MRS. CURTAIN snatches TOM's flask, kneels
down by ERNIE and tries to give him a drink from
it.)

MRS. C.   'Ere, mate. 'Ave a drop of faint restorer.
(She takes a swig herself.)

MARY   How did you manage to catch him?

MRS. LOTT   Over-arm smash. Like this.   (She demonstrates
with the racquet, narrowly missing TOM.)

TOM   Watch it!

CHRIS   (over the screen)   What about his gun?

MRS. LOTT   Water pistol.   (She squirts it over ERNIE, who
sits up spluttering.)

MRS. C.   (holding his head firmly)   There now. You're all
right. Lacey's got you. 'Ave a drink.

ERNIE   I don't want a drink.

MRS. C.   Do as yer flaming well told.   (She forces him to
drink from the flask. He splutters.)

ERNIE   Oh my gawd! I'd sooner be back in jail.   (He

	sees MISS BOUNCE and holds out his hands to be handcuffed.) Well, what are you waiting for? 'Urry up and arrest me for 'eaven's sake.
MISS B.	(coming forward) What for?
TOM	Drinking and drivelling.
MRS. LOTT	Causing an obstruction. He was poking something up the chimney next door.
ERNIE	I wasn't. I was looking for the money. (He points at CHRISTOPHER's head.) 'E said it was 'idden in the stove and it wasn't.
MRS. C.	(standing up and letting ERNIE's head fall to the floor with a thump) 'Ere! I 'ope you 'aven't been stuffing up our stove-pipes.
CHRIS	It must be there. I distinctly remember putting it in Hut Fourteen.
MARY	I thought this was Hut Fourteen.
	(MRS. CURTAIN finishes another crafty nip from the flask.)
MRS. C.	No, it ain't.
TOM	Fourteen's puce.
MRS. C.	And this 'ere's yeller. (She points at the bed rather wildly.)
ERNIE	(sitting up, rubbing his head) I swopped over the bedspreads.
CHRIS	Oh well, in that case I must have hidden the cash in here. It's in the stove – (He points at the stove and they all look at the smoke curling from it.) Oh no! You've lit the loot! (He emerges in underpants and pyjama jacket from behind the screen.)
ERNIE	(jumping to his feet) What!
	(MISS BOUNCE runs forward and restrains him.)
MRS. LOTT	It must have been hot money.
	(MRS. CURTAIN, now rather tipsy, points at CHRISTOPHER.)
MRS. C.	Droopy drawers.
	(CHRISTOPHER grabs the fire rattle from the

hook by the door and starts to make a terrible
din, jumping up and down, whirring the rattle
and shouting. He moves D.R.)

CHRIS   Fire! Fire!

              (MRS. LOTT puts her hands over her ears.
              MRS. CURTAIN finishes off the flask. MISS
              BOUNCE goes to the stove and she and TOM look
              solemnly inside. ERNIE, unnoticed, begins to
              edge towards the door U.R. TOM taps CHRIS-
              TOPHER on the arm and shakes his head.
              CHRISTOPHER rattles slower and slower and
              stops.)

TOM   Too late.

CHRIS   All those lovely fivers?

ERNIE   All gone?

              (TOM nods. MRS. LOTT hands CHRISTOPHER
              the golliwog.)

MRS. LOTT   Never mind. Have a consolation prize. We
              found him next door.

CHRIS   Oh golly! It's not the same.

              (MRS. LOTT unpins her hat and puts it on the
              bed. ERNIE makes a dash for the door, where
              he turns and shouts, shaking his fist.)

ERNIE   I've been robbed! Help! Police!   (He goes out
              and is seen crossing outside the window.)

MISS B.   (chasing after him)   Stop him! I am the police!

              (She goes out U.R. in hot pursuit. MRS. CUR-
              TAIN, now decidedly the worse for shock ab-
              sorber, staggers to the bed and sits down heav-
              ily.)

MRS. C.   Let 'im go! Hck! He's not the same as 'e was.
              'Is knees 'ave gone all knobbly. Hck! Pardon!

              (MARY suddenly flings her arms round CHRIS-
              TOPHER'S neck and hugs him.)

MARY   Darling!

CHRIS   What's that for?

MARY   You really are in Bubbles' hut by accident.

CHRIS   Of course I am. I kept telling you.   (He has been fidgeting with the golliwog and has extracted a piece of paper from inside it.)

MARY   Darling!

MRS. LOTT   (to CHRISTOPHER)   What have you got there, dear?

CHRIS   (reading)   It was inside the golliwog.   It says 'Number Thirteen, Lucky for Some.'

(MRS. CURTAIN jumps to her feet and steadies herself against TOM.)

MRS. C.   You've got it! Oops!

TOM   Yes, and you've had it. Hold up!

MRS. C.   You've won the Treasure 'Unt.

MRS. LOTT   Oh, what fun! What's the prize?

CHRIS   An extra week's holiday free. Ghastly!

MRS. LOTT   There! I knew it would all turn out right in the end.

(MRS. CURTAIN wambles down to the bathroom door D.L.)

MRS. C.   You've won the Jackpot. An extra week's 'oliday with everything laid on. Including our new Sandpiper 'Oliday Camp 'Ostess.   (She throws open the bathroom door.)   Tarar!

(In comes BUBBLES wearing feathers on her head, balloons in strategic places and precious little else.)

BUBBLES   (very seductively)   'Allo darleeng!   (She blows CHRISTOPHER a kiss and holds out her arms to him.)

CHRIS   Oh well! Who needs money?

(He takes a step towards her, arms outstretched, but MARY snatches the golliwog away from him and starts to belabour him with it.)

Ow! Stop it!

MARY   You wretch! You knew all the time!

CHRIS   No, I didn't! I swear! Mind golly! Ouch! Help!

(CHRISTOPHER starts to whizz the fire rattle again as MARY chases him round the stage

anti-clockwise. They go up and over the bed.
TOM pulls a large hat-pin from MRS. LOTT's
hat and, leering happily, starts to chase BUBB-
LES round the stage the opposite way. BUBBLES
screams and balloons burst. MRS. LOTT chases
TOM with the tennis racquet. The Tannoy bursts
into loud voice with 'I do Like to be beside the
Seaside.' HORACE dashes in U.R. blowing his
whistle, wearing a fireman's helmet and using a
garden spray in all directions.)

HORACE   Clickety click - sixty-six!

(MRS. CURTAIN jumps up on to the bed, waving
her flask.)

MRS. C.   Bingo!

(She starts to sing at the top of her voice. The
others join in.)

ALL   I do like to be beside the seaside.
              I do like to be beside the sea, etc.

ERNIE comes running in from the bathroom,
holding his skirts up and pursued by MISS BOU-
NCE who is clanging the Lights Out bell and
blowing her whistle. They weave through the
others and out of the door U.R.

The CURTAIN falls on a scene of complete
anarchy.

It rises again to disclose everyone in chorus
line across the stage, arms round one another's
waists doing high-kicks and singing loudly.

FINAL CURTAIN

PRODUCTION NOTE

From the first clang of Mrs. Curtain's boisterous entrance
to the anarchy and uproar of the Final Curtain this play must go
with a bustle and a swing. However unlikely the surroundings
of the Sandpiper Camp and whatever misfortunes befall the un-
suspecting campers, let the holiday spirit prevail! Colourful
costumes and bright stage dressing will help to counteract the
necessarily rather utilitarian setting but the main sparkle must
come from the pace of the acting and the vigour of the business.

Key man in the production is, of course, Christopher, who,
although perplexed by calamities mainly of his own making, must
retain throughout the sympathy of the audience. Guileless rather than gormless, he should appear a pleasant and affectionate
young fellow ill-equipped to cope with the troubles and tempt-
ations which beset him.

Mary is a straightforward character, attractive to look at
and genuinely fond of Christopher for all his foibles. Every now
and then she shows she is her mother's daughter, particularly
when Christopher appears to be slipping from her clutches, but
she must not be made too severe. And both she and Christopher
can be allowed to make the most of their occasional reconcilia-
tions.

Mrs. Lott herself is one of those larger than life characters we find organising outings for defenceless old folks who
would much prefer to be left in peace. She tramples through
life like an errant elephant with unremitting enthusiasm and a
fine disregard for the feelings of other people. An opportunity
here for some robust acting with, preferably, the appearance
to match.

Years of living in the midst of pother and ferment have en-
abled Tom to develop a protective stoicism. Long-suffering but
far from hen-pecked, he is, at heart, on Christopher's side and,
in spite of their apparent disagreements, we should be left in no
doubt that they are basically united against the wicked wiles of
women.

The actress playing Bubbles needs poise, presence and a

luscious figure. She shouldn't overdo the pseudo-French accent but use it to give the character that extra spice and stir the Old Adam (and perhaps the conscience) of every male heart in the audience. The basic Cockney can be allowed to re-emerge at moments of crisis.

And quite what Bubbles can see in Ernie Higgins we find it difficult to imagine. Sharp and ratty in thought and deed, a bucket on the head is just about what he deserves!

As for the three members of the 'staff' – Mrs. Curtain, Horace and Miss Bounce – all three must come across as real if eccentric characters. Mrs. Curtain should not be too shapeless and coarse – a heart of gold-leaf flutters somewhere beneath that grubby pinny; Horace, desiccated old drone that he is, can still be allowed a certain graveyard humour; and Miss Bounce, a cross between a gawky games mistress and a traffic warden, hides the makings of an attractive woman under that fierce exterior.

Staging and lighting should present few problems. The set could hardly be simpler and yet, with the minimum of adjustments between Acts, can easily suggest the change of location from hut to hut which is at the heart of the piece. The illusion can be enhanced by slight alterations in the position of bed and chairs but there should be no major change. The plot depends on our willing acceptance that Christopher, Tom and the others really do believe they are in their own hut.

The window U.L. needs to be large enough and low enough to allow Ernie to climb in and out without danger to himself or the set and to facilitate the various other bits of business that go on through the window. The cupboard D.R. should, if possible, give access to the wings to save Mrs. Curtain an uncomfortable quarter of an hour in Act Three.

Lighting is fairly straightforward. The main point to watch is that even when the light in the hut is 'out' there is enough light on stage (ostensibly from the lamp outside) to enable us to see clearly all that is going on. The shadow-play in Act Three is, of course, best achieved with a well-placed spot.

The smoke effect from the stove needs careful rehearsal to ensure the right amount at the right time. The disappearance of the whole company in a pea-souper, however reminiscent of last summer at the seaside, is not likely to provide a successful climax to the proceedings.

A word or two about Properties. The use of an undoctored fishing-rod in Act Two would present obvious dangers to

actors and the equilibrium of the set so, please, DO NOT USE
A HOOK of any description. A simple slip knot in the end of the
line will make it easy to attach and remove the 'catch' and may
prevent a nasty accident.

'Water, when poured, sprayed or squirted, should be used
with moderation. A little goes a long way and a soggy bed is not
much fun to lie in, particularly if your production takes place
during the winter. The screen should be of the folding variety,
big enough to conceal two refugees at a time but low enough to
allow Bubbles and Christopher to peer over the top when requir-
ed. It should have two small handles on the back to make it easy
for one person to lift and move about the stage.

Finally, and again for safety's sake, make sure poor Mrs.
Curtain can see where she is going when she emerges from the
cupboard. She will not serve the action well from the Orchestra
Pit.

JOHN DOLE

FURNITURE AND PROPERTY PLOT

ACT ONE

ON STAGE

Double bed (U. L.)
On it
Bedclothes
Pillows
Puce bedspread

Two small bed-side cup-
boards (L. and R. of bed)
In Left-hand cupboard
Two large tin mugs

Arm-chair (R. C.)

Two wooden chairs (one L.
of door U.R.; the other
L. C.)

Folding screen (R. wall)

Bright curtains (open)

Large cupboard (D. R.)
In it
Nude pin-up on door

Old print (R. C.)

First World War recruiting
poster (L. C.)

Large football rattle (Wall
R. of door U.R.)

Notice "Fire - Emergency
Only" (Below rattle)

Movable letters 'N' 'C' 'O'
on door D. L.

OFFSTAGE

In bathroom
Hand-towel (CHRIS)

Bath towel (BUBBLES)

Outside door U. R.
Movable number 'Thirteen'
on outside of door.
Fire-bucket partly filled
with water and marked
SAND - PIPER

Large Handbell (MRS. CUR-
TAIN)
Bag of golf-clubs (CHRIS)
Two tennis racquets (CHRIS)
Small fishing rod (CHRIS)
Haversack (CHRIS)
Car rug (CHRIS)
Golliwog (TOM)
Seaweed (TOM)
Small suitcase (BUBBLES)
In it
Shortie nightie
Magazine
Bottle of beer (CHRIS)
Large Bingo card
Attached to it: string
and pencil
Two large suit-cases
(HORACE)

PERSONAL

Whistle on string (HORACE)
Small piece of paper
(HORACE)
Two large lapel badges
(HORACE)
Handbag (MARY)
In it: handkerchief
Table-tennis ball (CHRIS)
Sun-glasses (CHRIS)
Cigarette (MRS. CURTAIN)
Bottle of gin (TOM)

ACT TWO

STRIKE

Puce bedspread
Print and poster
Pin-up in cupboard D.R.
Number 'Thirteen' from door
U.R.
Bucket
Slippers
CHRIS's hat
Tennis racquets
Blazer
Shirt
Magazine
Case
Towel
Golliwog
Sea-weed
Beer
Mugs
Handbell
Fishing rod (from cupboard D.R.)
Haversack   "   "   "
Car rug   "   "   "
Golf-clubs   "   "   "
Fur coat   "   "   "

CHANGE

Letters on door D.L. to read
"N.C.O."

SET

Yellow bedspread on bed
Photographs in frames (R.C.
and L.C.)
Larger nude pin-up in cupboard
D.R.
Fire-bucket outside door U.R.
Number 'Fourteen' on door U.R.
Half-empty bottle of gin on cup-
board R. of bed

OFFSTAGE

In bathroom

Two tooth-glasses (TOM and
CHRIS)

Black cash box (CHRIS)
In it
£5 Bank notes

Fishing rod (MARY)
Sou'wester (MARY)
TOM's clothes (MRS LOTT)
Golliwog (CHRIS)
Bikini top (CHRIS)
CHRIS's clothes (BUBB-
LES)
Bow, arrows and quiver
(HORACE)
Two table-tennis bats
(TOM)
Pail of unpeeled potatoes
(HORACE)

PERSONAL

Whistle on string (MISS
BOUNCE)
Riding crop (MISS BOUNCE)
Hip flask (TOM)
Wrist watch (TOM)
£5 Note (ERNIE)
Red spotted handkerchief
(HORACE)

ACT THREE

STRIKE

Yellow bedspread
Photographs (R.C. and
L.C.)
Nude pin-up in cupboard
D.R.
Number 'Fourteen' on door
U.R.
Bucket
Potatoes
Money
Cash-box
Tooth-glass
Hip flask
Table-tennis bats
Pyjama top and bottom

Bottle of gin
Arrow (from screen)
Bow

CHANGE

Letters on door D.L. to read
"N.O.C."

SET

Puce bedspread on bed
Picture and print as for Act
One
Pin-up in cupboard D.R. (as
for Act One)
Number 'Thirteen' on door U.R.
Candlestick, matches and enamel
mug on cupboard R. of bed
Tennis racquet on floor L. of
bed
BUBBLES' dress and under-
clothes on bed
Sea-weed over bed

CHECK

Fire-rattle in position U.R.

LIGHTS ON

DOOR U.R. OPEN

OFFSTAGE

In bathroom
Handbell (MISS BOUNCE)

Porter's truck (HORACE)
Blankets (HORACE)
Air-bed, half-inflated (HORACE)
Yellow bedspread (ERNIE)
CHRIS's pyjamas (ERNIE)
Number Board (Fourteen)
(ERNIE)
Playboy magazine (TOM)
Hot-water bottle (CHRIS)
In it – warm coffee
Tennis racquet frame (MRS.
LOTT)
Golliwog (MRS. LOTT)
In it:- small piece of paper
Garden spray (HORACE)

Fireman's helmet
(HORACE)

PERSONAL

Whistle (HORACE)
Muffler (HORACE)
Stethoscope (ERNIE)
Thermometer (ERNIE)
Water pistol (ERNIE)
Pipe (TOM)
Hip flask (TOM)
C.I.D. card (MISS
BOUNCE)
Whistle (MISS BOUNCE)
Hat pin (MRS. LOTT)

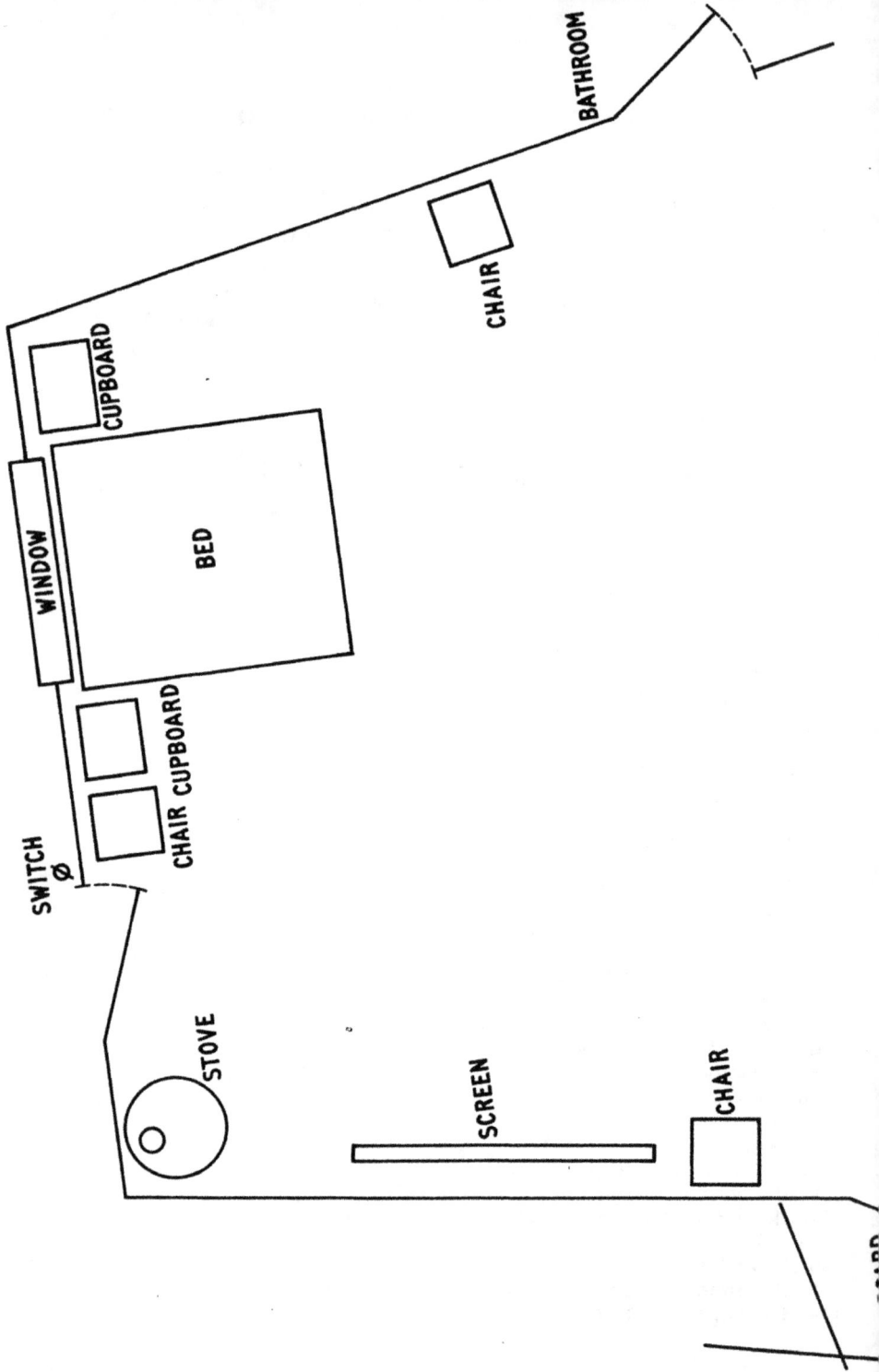

BATHROOM

CHAIR

CUPBOARD

WINDOW

BED

SWITCH
Ø

CHAIR CUPBOARD

STOVE

SCREEN

CHAIR

www.ingramcontent.com/pod-product-compliance
Lightning Source LLC
LaVergne TN
LVHW051747080426
835511LV00018B/3253